NRB L3/7

MW01016652

Clayton and Samson Mack, South Bentinck Arm, 1940.

GRIZZLIES & SASQUATCHES

from *Grizzlies & White Guys*

Clayton Mack

Clayton Mack, a Bella Coola Indian who died in May, 1993, at the age of 83, was renowned in hunting circles as the world's greatest grizzly bear guide. In fact, he was an all-round outdoorsman and heir to centuries of Bella Coola nature lore who fell into commercial guiding as a way of using his superb knowledge to earn a living in the white man's world, and often said he felt sorry for the animals he hunted because "they had no gun to shoot back." Mr. Mack's great compassion for other creatures of the wild as well as his celebrated skill as a storyteller is evident in the following accounts of his adventures with grizzlies, and with the legendary **Bookwus***, or Sasquatch.*

THE GUIDING BUSINESS

GRIZZLY BEAR GUIDING WAS GOOD business. I make a good living grizzly bear guiding. Get a new pickup truck every two years. Make a lot of good friends from all over. Americans and Germans. They give me lots of free gifts. Lots of things. Knives, guns, flares, rain gear, gumboots, clothes. I had about twenty rifles given to me, altogether, all my time guiding.

I see over three hundred grizzly bears get killed. I only shot the ones that tried to kill me or the wounded ones, that's all.

Once I got a guide licence, I could hire anybody I want. One year, around May, a bunch came in for a grizzly bear spring hunt. From Oklahoma. A grizzly bear nearly get me that first time. He hit me on the foot, tried to grab me. This was up Kwatna. We shot that grizzly bear on the tideflat, and he went up the mountain. One of the hunters was a millionaire, oil guy, Oklahoma oilman. This was the guy who shot the grizzly bear. I went and followed that bear's track and caught up to him and he charged us. So I shot, hit his front leg; kind of slow him down but he came, came again.

The hunter said, "Don't shoot. Let me finish him off."

"Okay, go ahead, but shoot quick," I said.

He start shooting and the bear keep coming. The bear went down. I got a stick and poked him in the lip, poked that grizzly bear in the mouth. He bite that stick, chop it in half like an axe. And he still breathing. Every time he turn his head I can see the steam, like, coming out of his nose.

"Quick, shoot him, finish him off. Shoot right in the neck behind the head," I said.

Bang! He shot him.

"I think he's dead," I said. "I think he's finished now." And I kick that bear in the ass end, kick it with my gumboots. He turned around and slapped me right on the toe, broke my toe. Then he fell down dead. Tough animal, that grizzly bear.

I was hunting in Owikeno Lake with three brothers. American boys. We came across the lake and I saw grizzly bear walking on the tide flats. At the Tzeo River, in that Washwash River country.

I took this kid, the youngest of the brothers. I was walking ahead of him and I saw a grizzly bear coming. A big one. Big grizzly bear! I stopped right away as soon as I saw it. "See that big grizzly bear coming?" I said. I stopped, never moved, just stand still. And there was a little baby grizzly coming behind her. I said, "Jack, it's a sow grizzly bear. Female. We don't shoot them. She's got a little baby. We can't shoot 'em. If we shoot the mother the wolves will kill the baby. They'll eat it up. That baby grizzly going to be sick for a long time, if he has no mother. Don't shoot her," I said. "Let 'em go."

So I stood in front of that grizzly bear and said, "Go on, beat it. Go on, bug off," I said. "I got a big gun, you don't want to get killed." The bear stopped and looked at me. She was about thirty feet away. She took off, took her little kid up a bank right into the heavy timber.

I said, "Let's go around, go circle around, hit the other creek. Get away from that cranky son-of-a-gun." Just as we started walking down to cut across to another creek we heard a stick breaking in the woods. "She's here already," I said. "She's on her way to the top of that bank. She try and run away too." I turned around to go back. I didn't know that it was a different bear, that one we heard on top of the bank breaking sticks.

Just as I started walking down the Washwash River, right where she turn around and went in the woods, that big grizzly bear sow, she came out of the woods. Full gallop. Not with her cub this time. She take that cub and hide it in the

woods and come back herself. She started snorting, I grab a rock and throw it right in front of her. It hit the water. She stood up on her hind feet. And I keep yelling at her, "Go on." That hunter was pointing his gun all the time. "It's all right," I said. "Don't shoot. Let me do the work," I said.

The bear keep coming toward me. She was gettin' pretty close now. I kneel down and I use my boy's gun. It's a big gun, .300 Winchester magnum. Big shells in it. I shot between the front legs. Hit the ground so the rocks will spray up into her stomach and make her run away. So I shot but the son-of-a-gun never, she never run away. Just keep coming. And I try and load again. If she makes one jump she'll reach me I thought. This time I going to shoot it in the head. I aim right between the eyes, like. *Bang!* I missed. I just burn the side of her head, one side. That bear come right after me. Jump, run and hit me on the side, left side. Threw me about twenty feet. She didn't slap me. I think she used her head. Run and hook me with her head like a cow, like a bull cow. That bear throw me quite a ways. I landed right

on my back.

I had too much stuff on my neck; I had binoculars, a camera, walkie-talkie and the big rifle. Too much in the way, like, I couldn't recover quick. I try to reload but she got me. She came, came right on top of me. I lay there, never move. Just keep still. She step on my one shoulder little bit with one foot, and she step on the other shoulder with the other foot. Put her nose right in my face. Kind of smell me, snorting, like. Saliva coming out of her mouth. I can smell that old rotten fish breath!

That hunter was kneeling down aiming at the bear. He shoot, *bang!* I hear that gun. She never bite me, I thought she was going to bite me right in the face. Funny, it don't bite. I don't know why it didn't bite. Then the blood came down. That young hunter, he shot right high in the neck, right on top of the neck. Cut the skin. And the blood drip all over my face and my chest. I can turn my head a little bit to watch that young hunter. He was aiming again. "Try and hit him in the ribs," I told him. "Shoot him right through the ribs, right through the lungs." He shot again, *bang!* and more blood came. Then the bear lay right on top of me. All that weight drop on top of me. Weigh about six hundred pounds. She just lay there, I couldn't move. She lay right on top of me, dead now. Blood just pouring out.

"Now, Jack, how you going to get me out?" I asked. "This son-of-a-gun weigh about a thousand pounds," I said. That young hunter try and move that bear off me but he can't do it. "Leave it for a little while maybe," I said.

He asked me if I can stand it.

"Yeah, I can stand it. You can run to the boys if you can't move it," I said. "Do you know where they are?"

"No, I don't know where they are," he said.

"Then leave this grizzly bear on me for ten minutes, maybe. Maybe it will get stiffened up, easier to roll it off then," I said. After a while I can feel it, that the bear startin' to get lighter. I get used to it maybe, get used to the weight on me. "Okay, push it, roll it to the right side," I said. By God, it rolled off. I get out of there quick. Blood all over my face.

We went to meet the other boys. "Bear got you, huh?" they ask.

"No, just lay on top of me, that's all," I said. Good story for them guys.

SASQUATCHES

I was fishing in Kwatna all by myself, in August, nobody with me, and I came home on the weekend. I was getting pretty lonely, low on gas, and getting low on grub too. So I went home for a few days. Then I got a fresh start of grub to go back again. I told my wife, "I'm going back to Kwatna again." Early in the morning, Sunday, I took off from Bella Coola.

I was probably in my thirties. I had a little boat, about a thirty-foot boat with a single cylinder engine. I got to Jacobson Bay, about fifteen miles from Bella Coola when I saw something right out on low tide. I saw something on the edge of the water. It was kneeling down, like, and I could see his back humping up on the beach. It looked like he was lifting up rocks or maybe digging clams. But there were no clams there. I turned the boat right in toward him, I wanted to find out what it was. For a while there I thought it was a grizzly bear, kind of a light colour fur on the back of his neck, like a light brown, almost buckskin colour, fur. I nosed right in toward him to almost seventy-five yards to get a good look.

He stood up on his hind feet, straight up like a man, and I looked at it. He was looking at me. Gee, it don't look like a bear, it has arms like a human being, it has legs like a human being, and it got a head like us. I keep on going in toward him. He started to walk away from me, walking like a man on two legs. He was about eight feet high. He got to some drift logs, stopped and looked back at me. Looked over his shoulder to see me. Grizzly bear don't do that, I never see a grizzly bear run on its hind legs like that and I never see a grizzly bear look over its shoulder like that. I was right close to the beach now. He stepped up on those drift logs, and walked into the timber. Stepped on them logs like a man does. The area had been logged before, so the alder trees were short, about eight to ten feet high. I could see the tops moving as he was spreading them apart to go through. I watched as he went a little higher up the hill. The wind blew me in toward the beach, so I backed up the boat and keep on going to Kwatna Bay.

One evening, a year later, I was talking to

4

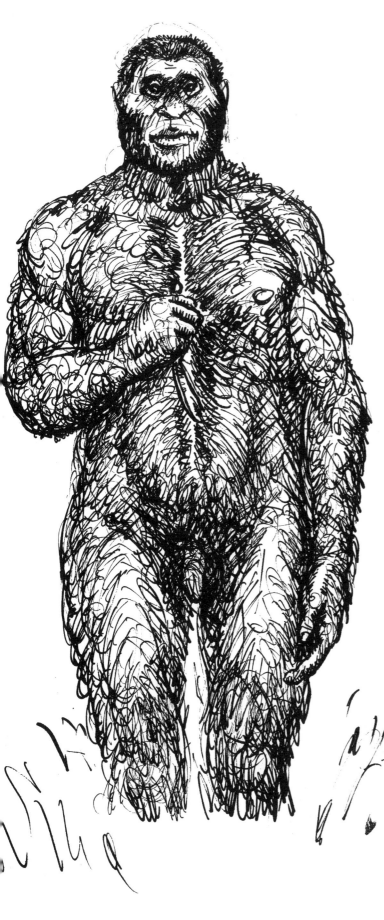

George Olsen, who was the manager of Tallio cannery. I told him about what I had seen, a man-like animal with hair all over his body. George told me he seen the same animal, the same month and the same year as I had, but only on the other side of the bay. George and his crew watched from their boat as a man-like creature run across the river.

For many years after, I told that story to people. I told Paul Pollard, James Pollard's father, and he told me where they are. Where is the most sasquatch sign he ever see. Kitlope! I wanted to get into that country someday to see if that is true. One June, I took two Americans into Kitlope. They had both got their grizzly bear, and wanted to see if they could see a sasquatch. One of these Americans, we called him Cowboy, was crying all the time and sometimes use bad language. Mad at something. When we get to Kitlope I said, "What is your problem?"

He said, "My wife left me. She cheated me and she wanted lots of money from me. She wanted thirty thousand dollars from me and she got it. Then she took off. A few days later I got a letter saying she wants sixteen hundred dollars a month for the rest of her life. And she got it." That's what he was mad about.

There was an old house at Kitlope. Oil stove, cups, dishes, plates, and spoons were all in good shape. I light up the stove. I called the boys to come in, "It's all ready for us."

Cowboy was still kind of haywire, you know, he pulled out a bottle of Canadian Club Whisky and a carton of cigarettes and put it on the table. Cowboy started right away, drinkin' and smokin'. He got me nervous, like, after a while. I was laying down watching him. He was smoking lot of cigarettes, he'd just finish one and then light a new one again. He keep going like that. Then he'd get up and go to the kitchen and pour himself a drink again. I watched him all the time. I decided next time he goes I would follow him and have a drink and help him forget his problem. Then he went in, and I went and patted him on the shoulder.

5

"I'll drink a drink with you on this one."

He said, "Take a big one, you are way behind."

"Damn right," I said. "I'll take a big one so I can go to sleep."

Poured himself a drink and poured myself a drink. I drink that Canadian Club whisky and go back to bed. I had my gun right there beside my bed and a big flashlight, a six-volt flashlight. I lay down, Cowboy started in again smoking. I never say nothing, just lay there watching him. Tony, the other American was laying near the foot of my bed on the next bed. I was afraid Cowboy was going to burn a blanket, burn down the whole cabin.

Right at once something yelled through a little broken window, *"Haaaaaaa ohhhhhh."* He yelled right through that hole in the window.

I get up right away and grabbed hold of my gun. That's the big mistake I made. I should have grabbed hold of that flashlight and flashed right on his face to see what he looked like. I grabbed my gun and I tried to go out but I couldn't open the door because it had been raining too long in that country, I guess, and the door swell up so I couldn't open it. So I went out through the back door, and flashed the light at the broken window. He was gone already. He yelled again by the river, he howl again, *"Haaaaaa ha ha ha haaaa,"* like. I flash around, it gone now. I walk down to the river to see if I can see him, what it was, but I didn't see nothing. So I went back to bed.

Early in the morning I wake up Tony. "Let's go look for his tracks," I said. Yeah, it looked like we saw his tracks, all right, but not too good. He stopped too many places. He destroy his own footprints. The footprints look like our footprints, big, that's all.

The second sasquatch I saw was in Mud Bay, in Dean Channel. Mud Bay is about ten miles down from Brynildsen Bay. It is like a kind of a lagoon there, narrow entrance to go in there but lots of room once you are inside. I was looking for bears. I didn't want to go into the middle of the bay, so I went to shore and walked along the sand beach. I see a man-head, it look like, behind a tree. It was looking at me. The head was sticking out from behind a tree. I kneeled down and point my gun at him. Gee, he took off fast. He was about two hundred feet away. Not too big, about my size—five foot seven or eight. Had lots of hair all over his face. Almost look like a person but not a person. I didn't want to shoot him. So I walked up to where he was. And where he went in I followed him. I saw a tree, bark had been peeled off. I guess, he was eating the sap of a hemlock tree. I almost caught him eating that. I saw tracks, but not too good.

The third sasquatch I saw was in South Bentinck, right up the head of South Bentinck. Past Taleomey, right at the end. Asseek River. It was less than twenty years ago. I had a white hunter with me, an American guy from California. Maybe fifty years old. We were sitting down on a log, talkin' together, he told me he's bad luck. There was a dead black bear near us. We found that dead black bear the week before and it had been eaten up by a grizzly bear. That American hunter shoot and missed a wolf, then later he shoot and missed a grizzly bear that come to eat that dead black bear.

He told me, "I'm real bad luck. I missed that wolf. I missed that grizzly bear. I just lost my son in the Vietnam War." His son just got killed in the Vietnam War. That's what he told me. We were waiting for the grizzly bear who was eating that dead black bear to come back. We waited till it gettin' dark.

It was starting to get dark so I told this guy, "It's getting late, let's get out of here. We'll be back before daylight in the morning." Sometimes when it gets late, when it's gettin' dark, and you shoot and you can't see the sights on the gun too good, you will just nick the bear. You won't kill him, just wound that bear. It's hard to track a wounded grizzly bear at night. So we headed back to the boat and I walk ahead of him. We got into a big open flat, about quarter of a mile. It looked like there was a black bear eating in the grass. Look like it anyways.

I stopped, I told this fellow, "Black bear over there, let's go right close to him, let's go walk right up to him." We were on the dry land about a hundred and fifty yards from the water. "Black bears are stupid," I told him. "You can get right close to them. See how close you can walk up to him." So I started walking up to that black bear. "Just stay right behind me," I told that American guy. The "black bear" was about a quarter of a mile away when we first saw it. I made a big circle like toward the bear. When I got closer, not too far now, the hunter grabbed the collar of my shirt and pulled me back.

"Clayton," he said, "that's not a black bear, that's a sasquatch." He keep on saying, "It's a sasquatch."

I didn't say nothing, I started walking again. I said, "Stay right behind me." He was only about seventy-five yards away.

"Clayton," he said again, "that's not a black bear, that's a sasquatch."

I kneel down on the ground, I turned toward him, "What do you know about sasquatch?"

He says, "I come from North California, we get them in that country. In the big mountains that get snow on them. Those mountains in Northern California which have glaciers on them. Some people hunt them," he said.

I said, "How do they look like?"

He said, "Well, you seeing one there now, that's how they look like!"

And I started walking again. I get pretty close, now. Then that "black bear" stand up on his both legs, and he look at me. I keep going closer. Gee, I was pretty close now. He started looking at me, make no noise or anything. I feel the barrel of a gun against my cheek. I pushed that hunter's gun away from my face. "Don't shoot him," I said.

That hunter whispered in my ear, "Look through your scope and see how he look like."

I turned the scope to 4X — wide and close — four times closer than naked eye. I looked through that scope, I look at his mouth. Little white thing in his mouth, look like rice. I look at

his lips kind of turnin' in and turnin' out, the top and the bottom, too. I look at his face and his chest. The shape of his face is different than a human being face. Hair over face. Eyes were like us, but small. Ears small, too. Nose just like us, little bit flatter, that's all. Head kind of look small compared to body. Looks friendly, doesn't look like he's mad or has anything against us. Didn't snort or make sound like a grizzly bear. On the middle of his chest, looked like a line of no hair, hair split apart little bit in the middle. Skin is black where that hair split apart. It was a male, I think. I can't — no way I can — shoot him. I had a big gun too. Big gun, .308. I aim, had my finger on the trigger, point it right at the heart. One shot kill him dead, just like that. I couldn't shoot him. Like if a person stand over there, I shoot him, same thing. No way I can kill him.

My mother told me, "Don't ever kill sasquatch, don't shoot 'em. If you shoot 'em, you gonna lose your wife, or else your mother or your dad or else your brother or sister. It will give you bad luck if you shoot them, kill them. Leave them alone," she said. "If you see one, walk the other way, let them walk that-a-way." That's why I don't want to shoot one. My mother had seen them. She hear them too. A lot of Indian people seen them in the old days.

After we see it, we just leave it. That sasquatch went in the woods, went in the big timber. He took off fast. Looked like he used his hands when he took off first, like a hundred yards runner, looks like it. Pulling himself up with his arms, with his hands, looks like it. He never make a sound. Just ran into the heavy timber like a fast-moving shadow.

Next day we had a look again, around where that sasquatch was eating. We wonder to ourselves, "What was he eating?" He pull that grass, and right at the root of the grass is a little round seed. Look's like a little piece of rice. That white boy called it sweetgrass. That was what he was eating. That was the last sasquatch I saw, but I hear lots of stories about sasquatch. I was happy that American hunter from California saw a

Clayton Mack at Kwatna, 1940.

sasquatch. He was happy he saw a sasquatch.

I used to own a big boat. One time I took a basketball team to Ocean Falls, Bella Bella and Klemtu. Took about twenty-five boys on it. They hired me to do this. I have to be careful, don't travel in the bad weather or else you get in trouble, sink and lose that many boys. I was coming back from Klemtu, it was getting late, we get past Brynildsen Bay and we hit a strong wind blowing out from South Bentinck. I turn the boat around and go back to Brynildsen Bay. We going to wait till it is nice and take off to Bella Coola in the morning. The boys didn't like that, they wanted to go home that night. "No, I'm the boss,"

I said. There was too many of us in the boat. I hear sasquatch live in that bay area. Willie Hans got to the bow of boat and tied up the boat good. I cooked something to eat. We plan to leave early in the morning before the wind come up.

Art Saunders, he yelled at Willie Hans, "Sasquatch."

Willie Hans raised his head up high and said *"Baaaa qaaa,* are you there?"

Sasquatch answer right away, *"Haii haii haii."* Just like he call his name in our language. We call him *Boqs.* The thing answered right now. The whole works, jam in the door—they can't squeeze through the door fast enough. That was about fourteen years ago.

I also hear sasquatch in Skowquiltz River valley. Not too long ago, a hunter and his wife came in. I took him to South Bentinck. He was a poor shot, he can't hit nothing with his gun. Good gun too, twelve hundred dollar gun. I show him a black bear, *bang, bang,* he miss. Show him a grizzly bear, *bang, bang,* missed all the time. He can't hit anything. We talk about sasquatch one day.

"Ah, bullshit," he said. "No such thing as that in the world." He asked me how it look like.

I told him about the black one I saw in South Bentinck. Look like human being, body like human being.

He said, "It's all bullshit."

His wife get mad at him. "Don't call it bullshit," she said. "You never see one in your life that's why you don't believe? I bet you never see a wolf too." She was right, he never did see a wolf in the wild. I tried to get him a bear in South Bentinck, we did see a lot of bears but he can't hit them — missed all the time.

I told my son-in-law, "Let's go to Skowquiltz. It's easy to hunt there, easy hunting, lot of black bears there."

So we went to Skowquiltz River valley. It was getting late in the evening when we get there. Starting to get dark. I took this guy out and I sat down on a log, waiting for a bear to come out. I saw one right away, quick. A black bear, he wanted to cross the meadow in front of us.

"There's a black bear over there now, do you see it?" I asked him.

"Yeah, let's go look," he said. We went to a meadow waiting for the bear but he never did show. Lots of bear sign, ground all dug, but no bears. We went back to the same log and sat down again. A sound scared us. Real awful noise. Looks like a bluff up above, where the sound come from, *Awwwoooo wooo wooo.* That sasquatch was talking but I couldn't understand what he was saying. Real deep voice.

The hunter asked me, "What's going on over there?"

"You don't believe in sasquatch?" I said, "That's one now! You hearin' one now, you still don't believe it? That's what it is. Maybe lost each other, trying to call its mate, maybe it's his wife he's trying to call."

No answer though, just a big deep voice. Awful sounding voice. Scare me, usually I not scare in the woods. As long as I have my gun, I'm not afraid. But that voice sure scared me. I start thinkin' maybe it's a ghost or spirit or something like that. Cougar don't sound the same as sasquatch, I can tell the difference. Porcupine sounds like a woman crying sometimes, but that sasquatch cry is different than porcupine.

My brother saw a sasquatch. My brother Samson. Standing face to face, about a foot and half apart! He was on the tideflats here. He was working the boom there. Early shift in the morning, fire season, had to go across to the other side, the Old Townsite side, at about three o'clock in the morning. Samson meet that sasquatch right on the road. Samson stopped, the sasquatch stopped and they looked at each others. And Samson, he wouldn't tell anyone about it for a long time.

Sometimes I wonder what kind of animal is a sasquatch. Half man, half animal, I think. Just like a man but can't make fire, that's all. You know all the Indians up and down coast have the same name for sasquatch, *Bookwus* or *Boqs.* Many different languages, but same name for sasquatch. I think they live in caves in the winter, hibernate like a bear. I don't think they like fish. Sasquatch got strong smell, smell like a pig they say. I never smell it, never did in my life. But a lot of guys smell them. They see them and smell them. I saw the one in South Bentinck up close, but I never smell nothing on him. Maybe wind blowin' the other way.

The way a sasquatch finds out how far apart each others is, is they pick up a stick and hit a tree with that stick. Makes a spooky noise. You will hear *bong* on one side of a valley, then *bong* when another one answer from the other side of the valley.

There are sasquatch hunters, quite a bunch

of them. They try and get a sasquatch. Some sasquatch hunters come and see me. One guy say to me, "You tell me where I can get a picture of a sasquatch. If I can get it, I get 125,000 dollars."

"What you going to do with that picture?" I asked him. "Make millions of copies of it, and kids they will buy that and put it on their shirt," he said. He stay with me for awhile.

Look like there is a lot of money in that sasquatch hunting business. I want to join them someday. One day that sasquatch hunter, he need some money to buy grub to go back in the mountains. He was hunting back of Salloomt River valley. He want to buy oranges for bait. He claim that sasquatch likes apples and oranges. He going to scatter them all over his camp. He didn't have any money to buy this stuff he wanted. So he said, "Can I use your phone?"

"Yeah, okay," I said.

And he phoned a guy in Agassiz, who was hunting sasquatch too. He get through to the guy. I hear him say he needs over eight hundred dollars, he tells that guy to send the money to the Credit Union here. He get it just like that! Over a thousand bucks by the time he trade in his American money for Canadian money.

I think there is still a few sasquatch families around. Up the Talchako River, Kitlope River, Skowquiltz River, and in South Bentinck. They travel long ways, cover a lot of ground in a day. I think someday someone will get a sasquatch. I could have got one long ago if I wanted to kill one. I just couldn't kill it. I couldn't kill one for a million dollars. A sasquatch looks too much like a man.

I hope they don't log the Skowquiltz. Lucky to get three million feet of logs out of that country. Leave it to the sasquatches. I hope they don't log the Kitlope too. There's not much logs in there either. Leave them rivers alone. That Kitlope is mountain goat, grizzly bear, moose, and black bear country. Lot of black bears in there. Skowquiltz, Koeye and Kitlope Rivers. Those are some of the last ones.

Any grizzly bear and salmon river or creek around, them loggers go in there and get the trees. Ashlulm, Aseek, Bella Coola, Cascade, Chuckwalla, Clyak, Dean, Eucott Bay, Frenchman Creek, Genesee, Inziana, Jenny Bay, Johnstone, Kilbella, Kimsquit, Kwatna, Larso Bay, Machmell, Milton, Namu, Necleetsconnay, Neechanz, Nicknaqueet, Nieumiamus, Noeick, Nooseseck, Nootum, Quatlena, Sheemahant, Taleomey, Tzeo, Wannock, and the Washwash River. They all been logged.

Why does the government have to kill so many trees and kill them so fast? Trees been there hundreds and hundreds of years, why them white guys want to cut them all down in less than fifty years? What is the rush? Why are those white guys so damn greedy? Why does the government want to do that to all the grizzly bear and salmon river valleys?

From *Grizzlies and White Guys*, by Clayton Mack and Harvey Thommasen, Harbour, 1993.

VISITORS

Dick Hammond

ONE FINE DAY TOWARD THE END OF summer in 1907, one of the girls came running up from the beach. "Mother, Father, someone's coming in a boat!" Everyone stopped what they were doing and in a few minutes the whole family was on the floating dock watching a strange boat approach.

Hidden Basin was as secluded as its name suggests. Visitors were few, and strangers rarely found their way through the narrow channel into the basin. When someone did, it was an occasion of considerable excitement.

As it came closer, they saw a rowboat about fourteen feet long with one man sitting in the stern while another rowed from the middle seat. The boat slipped cleanly through the calm water, as boats did when one might have to row fifty miles or more in one. A double row of swirls made by the oar blades stretched out behind.

"Nice lines," said Jack Hammond approvingly. "Looks like an Andy Linton." (One of the best boatbuilders of that time.)

As the oarsman eased the boat alongside the float, they saw that he was a youth of about fourteen or sixteen years, but tall and well built. He didn't reply to Jack's greeting, but smiled at them all in a friendly way. He jumped lightly onto the float and knelt to tie up the boat, still without a word. Jack held out his hand to the older man in the stern seat to assist him onto the float, but he was completely ignored. The man just sat there with a slight smile on his lips, his eyes oddly unfocussed. Cliff and Hal watched with a mixture of delight and trepidation. Their father was not a patient man; certainly not one to be treated like this on his own float. His face was beginning to redden with that temper which they all feared. Just then the youth uttered some weird bird-like chirps and whistles, at the same time snapping his fingers in a sort of pattern, and just in time the older man turned toward them and spoke.

"Friends," he said in a gentle voice, "I can hear you but I cannot see you. The Lord has seen fit to take away my sight. I am Father _____, and my young companion and helper here is Jeremiah, or Jerry for short. We bring the word of God to those who wish to listen. Our aim is to visit every isolated homestead and cabin on the coast, if the Lord should see fit."

Jack Hammond was delighted. He had at one time been intensely religious, but his restless mind had led him to the works of Darwin, whose theories he had accepted with complete conviction. However, unlike their originator he didn't believe that Darwinism and religion could co-exist. One of his greatest pleasures was to corner some man with strong religious beliefs and proceed to demolish them with the aid of copious references to the Bible, natural history and Darwin, on which subjects his knowledge was encyclopedic. Thus he greeted the unsuspecting priest with an enthusiasm to which he was probably not accustomed, insisting that he come for dinner and stay the night at least. There were, he confided cunningly, a few passages in the Bible that he would like to have clarified.

"My boys will take care of Jeremiah. You Hal, Cliff, take the lad and show him around."

"Ah, you have boys; good. I'm sure Jerry will get along well with them. He is a most good-natured soul. There is just one thing I must mention. As God made me sightless, so he took away Jeremiah's voice. He can hear, but he cannot speak."

Surely no stranger pair has travelled this coast. A blind priest and a mute boy. Not quite the halt leading the blind, but close!

Cliff and Hal were horrified. Wary of strangers at best, they were appalled by the prospect of entertaining one with some sort of disability. They felt no sympathy, even less considering the other was several years older, a vast gap at that age. But under the watchful eye of their father they had no choice but to beckon him to come along. They walked along the shore, glancing furtively at Jerry, who followed a few paces behind. He was a head taller than them, with long black hair and a tanned face. His big hands dangled at the ends of long arms that seemed even longer, for his tattered coat was made for a much smaller man. About eight inches of wrist hung bare out of each sleeve. The same was true of his trousers, which ended about halfway between knees and ankles. With the ill-fitting clothes and the grin that he still wore as he looked around him, they were sure he wasn't anyone they wanted to know.

"Let's lose him," hissed Cliff to his brother. They walked a bit faster, increasing the distance between them and the strange youth. When they were out of sight of the house, they dashed behind some boulders and through the bushes, and cut away from shore running as fast as they could go. Then they hid behind a tree watching the beach. Soon Jeremiah came ambling along, looking around for his companions.

Cliff took a rock out of his pocket. They were never without a few throwing rocks, being always on the lookout for good ones. "Watch this." With an easy, practised motion he flung the rock. It was a good throw; the rock hit the water not far from the stranger. But much to their

surprise, instead of being alarmed, he looked up and grinned a great pleased grin.

They had concealed themselves behind the tree as soon as the rock took flight, so that little more than their eyes showed. They felt quite safe. Jerry looked slowly around him. He put his hand in his pocket. As he took it out again he flicked his arm in a careless-seeming way, and there was a loud *thwack* from the tree behind which Cliff and Hal thought they were hidden. A piece of bark flew from a spot about a foot over their heads

and dropped into the bushes.

The boys were profoundly shocked. The ease and accuracy of that throw presented a challenge such as they had never imagined. They were vain about their rock-throwing. They had been at it since they were big enough to pick up a rock, and they threw at every opportunity at anything that presented itself. They threw until their arms ached, and then they threw some more, until their accuracy and range with a good rock were phenomenal. So good that they hunted grouse and ducks with rocks, with considerable success. Which was the more remarkable because their father would not tolerate bruised meat and they must hit their quarry on the head. As for range, they had recently routed a gang of five older boys on an outing to Whaletown—whose youths were implacably hostile to strangers—without a single enemy rock landing near them.

So war was declared on the peaceful shore of Hidden Bay. Both sides were enthusiastic at first, but it soon became apparent to one side that they were badly outgunned. However stealthily they might crawl, when they raised their heads a rock would whistle by their ears with a velocity they could scarcely believe. No ambush worked, no plan of attack came even close to succeeding. It was the most frustrating afternoon of their lives. Jerry had eyes in the back of his head, an arm like a catapult and the ability to read minds. And to make matters worse, his face never for a moment lost that delighted, infuriating grin.

At last came the sound of the supper bell. An armistice would have to be declared. From a place of safety Cliff called, "Come on, it's suppertime." They cut home through the woods, leaving Jerry to find his way back however he could, and his long legs brought him to the door at almost the same moment as they arrived. They watched him enter, feeling more than a little apprehensive, as well as a bit guilty. They needn't have worried. He appeared as friendly as ever, as if he had thoroughly enjoyed a pleasant and playful afternoon.

Dinner was the signal for the cessation of another combat of quite a different kind, if no less hard-fought. The priest had proven a most formidable opponent for their father, whose absent-minded replies to any question at dinner indicated that he was using the truce to marshal arguments for the fray which would certainly begin again after the meal. But now, as they ate, there was lighter conversation. News from down the coast and gossip of all sorts, at which their visitor also appeared adept. The girls chattered, the brothers were almost as mute as their guest.

The evening passed quickly, and the philosophical discussion ended inconclusively as such affairs tend to end. At last the sleeping arrangements were organized and the house was still.

After breakfast the visitors prepared to leave. Provisions were pressed on them, and advice on what they would encounter, who would welcome them, whom to avoid or risk being shot at!

Down at the dock there were a few last words of discussion. The priest said mildly, "Well, you have a point there, I must admit. But God can give as well as take away. Jeremiah, now, might serve as an example." Turning to the youth, he said, "Show them your skill, Jeremiah."

Jeremiah grinned his ready grin. He picked up a piece of bark about the size of a man's hand, and with an easy motion tossed it in a long arc high over the bay. As it rose, he put his hand in his pocket and threw again. A rock sped almost too fast to see. There was a sound like a handclap as the piece of bark exploded into fragments at the top of its trajectory.

"Show them, Jeremiah," said the priest again.

The youth dug into his pocket. Then he threw with that odd jointed motion they had seen him use. It was the first time they had seen him appear to exert himself. A rather large rock flew out over the bay. They waited for it to drop, but instead of dropping it continued to rise, and rise, until their eyes could not longer track it. In that sheltered windless bay the water was glass-smooth, and to the astonished watchers there appeared no splash, no sound. Did it go—incredibly—right across the bay? They would never know.

Their father said slowly, "That is the most extraordinary display I have ever seen. However, I do not concede the point."

The priest laughed. "I didn't think you would!" he said. He offered his hand, which was taken very cordially. Goodbyes were said, and in a few more minutes the boat was sliding smoothly down the bay.

The boys stood alone on the float after the others had left. They were stunned. It was quite apparent that they had been at the mercy of the incredible Jeremiah all during that day of mock war. Mock on his side, at any rate. They felt strangely humbled. Jack Hammond said later, "You see, up until then we thought we could do anything that anyone could. That if we really tried, we could do better. But there on that beach, we knew in our hearts that we could never, with any amount of practice, do what he could do so easily. We were never quite the same, ever again."

The boat was by now about a hundred yards from the float. Jerry was facing them as he rowed. Suddenly, as if by the same impulse, Cliff and Hal both waved to him. As he completed his stroke, he let go the oars and stood. His arm moved and a rock sped humming between them as they stood there just a few feet apart. It smacked into the water behind them and went skipping up along the beach. As he sat down again, Jerry waved back at them gaily. They had a sense of something lost, that would never be found again.

Next day the weather changed, and that night the first of the fall storms sent southeast winds howling up the gulf. A week or so later, on a chance meeting with a settler from Texada Island, Jack asked for any news of the strange pair, as their intended route led his way, but the man had seen nothing of them. Neither had anyone else in the area, as Jack gradually met and queried them. Nor did he ever find anyone who had met them after that day when they had left Hidden Bay. As far as Jack could discover, they were never seen again.

A horse-drawn wagon splashes through high tide on Saturna, back when the only road was the beach.

SATURNA

Barry Brower

ABOUT FIVE THOUSAND YEARS BE-fore ferry lineups and tourist hotels, the Coastal Salish people visited the Gulf Islands to hunt, fish for salmon and gather camas bulbs and berries. They had the place pretty much to themselves until the 1790s when the topgallants of British and Spanish sailing ships appeared on the horizon. Many island place names reflect the arrival of European explorers. Saturna Island, at the southern extreme of the Gulf Islands, was named after the Spanish naval vessel *Saturnina*, which passed through the area in 1791. Narvaez Bay, on the island's southeast side, was named after the ship's commander, José Maria Narvaez.

Non-Indian inhabitants, primarily British,

began arriving in the 1850s and all of the major islands in the group had settlements of whites by the 1870s. According to the Provincial Archives publication *The Gulf Islanders*, "pioneering in the Gulf Islands was a mild experience when compared to the grueling, backbreaking, and soul-destroying activity it was in many other parts of British Columbia. . . . They were on a well-travelled transportation route between Victoria and the Lower Mainland of British Columbia [and] did not become 'bushed' since they could simply flag the next steamer and be in Victoria, New Westminster, or Vancouver within two or three hours."

Small-scale farming, orcharding and dairy

farming were all attempted in the early days, but the thin soil of the islands, transportation problems and economic competition from other areas of the province undermined most of the settlers' best efforts. Sheep ranching on grassy, craggy ridges, and fishing are the enduring enterprises from pioneer times, and many islanders now depend on tourism directly or indirectly for some portion of their income.

One exception is Dave Jack. Dave, his wife Flo and their adopted son Mike live in Boot Cove, a quiet little bay on the northern end of Saturna Island. They occupy a modest frame home spilling over with the physical and pictorial remains of Dave's half century of boatbuilding, steam-engine tinkering, logging and fishing. A cluttered yard, boatbuilding shop, garden and outbuildings give way to an extensive patchwork docking facility which is frequently mistaken for a public marina. A constantly changing flotilla of boats anchor here — sailboats, fishing boats, clinker-builts — some belonging to Dave, others temporarily moored for repair or storage. The only indication that these are private facilities is a small hand-lettered sign announcing there is "no store."

The house has an orange front door scratched deeply by a rusty horseshoe knocker, and most days a tap on it will produce at least one member of the Jack family. Today it is Dave in a green work shirt and Rodeo Rambler pants lashed snugly by a black leather belt. The belt is too long for his waist and the excess end dangles loosely in front of him.

An independent, resourceful sort (a "rough-cut diamond" is how one islander describes him) of medium height and build, Dave has an earthy presence accented by a slightly cocked glass eye, the result of a World War Two accident.

Inside, Dave likes nothing better over a mug of tea or coffee than to tease, shock and generally entertain visitors with crusty and mischievous tales of his time in the Gulf Islands. This day Dave is feeling particularly frisky. Fortified by a couple of jiggers of Canadian rye whisky, he is reminded of an incident that happened on Saltspring Island years ago. In the background Flo chuckles and fills in details while Dave tells about the time he knocked a chimney off a house — with his boat.

Island Rover off Monarch Head, ca. 1988.

Jack Family at Gordon Head, ca. 1937. David Jack is third from left.

"I was working on a boat of mine at the time and this young fellow, Harvey Sylvester, came running down and he says, 'Dave, any chance of you taking me to Ganges? My wife's gonna have a baby.' I said, 'Okey-dokey,' any excuse to go to Ganges. We were off like a shot. I went out to the *Saturna Maid* and starts her up and rushes off to Ganges. I tried to go in on the old provincial wharf and suddenly the boat veered off toward a plane that was tied up there. I thought, 'What the hell, I never turned the wheel!' I continued to veer and just at that moment I looked up and noticed that a chimney on a house there fell off. I went astern and just missed the plane. I looked up again and the picket fence by the house was going down like dominoes. I could see shrubs turning up, and dust. I couldn't figure out what the hell was going on. So all of a sudden I could hear people shouting 'Whoa! Stop her!' And just at that point I saw this forty-foot pole with an antenna on it go by the boat. It had been located on top of a piling on the wharf and the antenna was connected by a wire to the chimney. This guy came down from the house and said, 'You're gonna have to pay for that!' I said, 'That's navigable waters you spread that across there. It's not my fault.' I walked uptown to pick up some items and as I walked by the old provincial police office Roy Whitehead

came running out and he says, 'Dave, just a minute, I don't know what's going on but I was told to stop you.' I said, 'Oh, there's nothing wrong. I just knocked a chimney off the BC Airlines house with my boat.' He started to laugh and I said, 'Yeah, that damn antenna they got there, I went and clipped it with my bow poles and took the chimney off.' Roy couldn't stop laughing. So after a while I headed up to the pub and when I was going down to the boat later here comes Roy and he says, 'Oh, Dave, I got somethin' funny to tell you. The BC Airlines guy thought you should have to pay but I looked it up'—he started to laugh again—'and it comes under an act of God.'"

David Stirling Jack was born October 6, 1925 in North Vancouver. Dave's father, Melville Jack, was born in Scotland. He was a skipper and officer on the Canadian Pacific Railway's coast fleet of passenger ships. A deep sea navigator, he helped to bring the Princess fleet of ships (the *Marguerite*, *Kathleen* and *Elaine*) from the shipyards in Scotland to British Columbia. In about 1930 the family moved to Victoria and then Pender Island before moving back to Scotland in 1938. In 1943 Dave returned to British Columbia and worked as an apprentice boatbuilder at both the Armstrong and Foster shipyards in Victoria.

The great day. **Island Rover** *ca. 1977.*

Soon dissatisfied, Dave decided, "To heck with it, I'm going to build a boat," and promptly moved to Saturna Island.

"I learned to build by common sense," he remembers. "That's all. God, anybody could build a boat. There was a little sawmill in Winter Cove in those days and they would saw the logs and give you half. That's how I got all the planking and all the parts and pieces for the boat. I built the *Saturna Maid* in 1947, the *Aeolus* in 1959, the *Saturna Rose* in 1964 and the *Island Rover* in 1977. We built each of these for ourselves. Ten years is as long as we would keep a boat. After that we would sell it and build another one. Now, the *Aeolus*, that was about the craziest thing I could ever have done. Too big. Too clumsy. Forty-five feet by a fourteen-foot beam and she drew seven feet of water. Not a handy boat for doing anything, you know. If you ever saw a rock or a sign of bottom, boy, it was too late then. You'd already hit."

Dave Jack's concern with the impact of form on function extends to his interest in steam-powered craft. Steam engines fascinated him as a youth in Scotland, and he often went to visit his brother at an engine-building yard. His uncle had a lathe and Dave built his first steam engine at the time. Today, steam engines and parts are to be found all over Dave's property—in his basement, shop, yard, even the living room—and his current boat, the *Island Rover*, has already had two steam engines in it, though he is currently using a more conventional diesel model.

While Dave Jack is clearly comfortable entertaining visitors at the kitchen table with humorous anecdotes and recollections of island events and people, Flo Jack maintains a low-key presence as she moves about the kitchen and house, periodically interrupting to supplement or correct Dave's reminiscences. These stories are probably many times retold, but Flo seems as genuinely interested in them today as she was when they occurred. She has a broad, flat smile and a jolly laugh, and one senses in some of Dave's stories a kidding, playful, almost childlike

Flo Jack in 1957.

bond between the two.

"Let me tell you the story about the rotten apples. We used to keep our apples in a big long shed we had and pull them up in a line along a tray so the mice couldn't get at them. So anyway, I climbed up and was lookin' for rotten apples and I was tryin' to throw them out the end of the shed. Flo was down below and one of them hit a beam, bounced off and landed right on top of her head and went *sploosh!* Oh, she was mad! She said, 'For Christ's sake, watch where you're throwin' them apples!' She moved somewhere else and I threw several more and then one of them hit her right on the shoulder. She said, 'That's it!' She started heavin' rocks at me. I couldn't dodge them up there so I beat it. I jumped down on the deck of this schooner I was buildin' and jumped off the bow. She chased me around the bow and around the stern and then into the cabin. Now, in the cabin the door opened outwards. I pulled the door shut and was just goin' to put the hook on the door and she grabbed it and— *uuumph!*—pulled me right off my feet! I sailed out with the door, which got torn clean off the hinges, landed on the ground, and I couldn't breathe. There I lay. It was absolutely an accident! I never tried to hit her. She still won't believe it."

Flo Jack was born Flo Howard on the Alberta prairies. Her family moved to Saltspring Island when she was young and her father farmed a plot of land there. It was hard making a living on Saltspring, and isolation was a problem, particularly in the winter months, but there were parties and get-togethers and it was at one of these events that Dave Jack and Flo Howard met for the first time.

"I played the guitar a little bit," Dave recalls. "I knew Flo's brother and one day he said, 'C'mon Dave, I want you to take my mother and sister over to a dance on Pender.' So I goes up to his house and I meets this nice-looking chickadee, and she's washing eggs. We headed off for the dance and it was quite a dance. The dances lasted all night in those days. So of course I was sniffin' around her place steady after that. Every Saturday night we'd bugger off. Nobody ever knew where we went. I mean, Christ-amighty, when you go to buy a pair of shoes in a shoe store you don't look at the shoes on the shelf and say, 'Well, I think they might fit me, I'll buy 'em!' Don't you always try a shoe first?"

The "shoe" apparently fit well, for it wasn't long before the two decided to get married. "I went over to Ganges to pick up Flo in a little boat I called the *Snoose*. We were on our way back and it was gettin' quite dark and we were just off Long Harbour and I leans over to her and I says, 'Let's get married!' And, don't you know, I reached over to the wooden tiller and it came out of my hand and the rudder fell off the boat and we had no steering! The minute I asked her to marry me! We never did find the rudder. So I lost my steering from then on."

The two were married in 1956 and, listening to Dave, one soon learns that adventures of this sort have been commonplace ever since. "In these little old cabins we used to have, you had a sink and you just ran a rubber hose through a hole in the floor and it drained to a hole in the ground we dug and filled with stones. One day I went out to the shop behind the cabin and looked down the hole and it looked like there was lots of rats in it.

Dave takes advantage of a lull in the fishing to play a tune on his accordion, 1951.

*Dave Jack built the **Saturna Maid** at Boot Cove in 1947.*

I had some naphtha gas and I poured it down the hole and sauntered into the house and got a box of matches. I was sitting on the bank above the hole with a big stick in case a rat came out. I'm throwing these matches trying to hit the hole and geez, I couldn't hit that hole. Finally, one hit it. When the match hit the hole it made a noise like a rumbling roar in a steel pile. Two things happened. There was a scream came out of the kitchen, and an old rat came running out of the hole burning and it ran toward me where there was a big pile of lumber. There was a bunch of dry leaves on the lumber and it set fire to them. The scream so unnerved me that I never swung the stick at the rat. Flo came running out of the house and said, 'What the hell are you doing?' She had been standing in front of the sink and out of the sink bowl came this flame and it went straight up and hit the ceiling! Right in front of her nose! Gee, she was mad. I tell you we were never bothered with rats again."

While many Saturna residents have similar adventures to tell, life has not been easy for everyone. There are few services and no industry, and agriculture is difficult because of the thin soil. A few people fish seasonally, but others have to scrape out a living where they can find it—a short-term government job here, a little carpentry there, maybe some unemployment insurance now and then. And there are those who come to Saturna with enough money that they don't have to worry about it. Still, Dave will tell you that many people arrive on the island with high expectations—and soon leave.

"There's no work here. You have to have money to come here or be retired. There's not much of a back-to-the-land thing either. And people want a ferry every ten minutes. You ought to be here in the winter. The ferry will go back and forth three or four times and not a soul's been on it. People on this island don't run to town every day. A ferry twice a week would be quite appropriate. We don't have police. We don't need them. If people get mad enough they'll get a bunch together and settle it themselves. If there's a medical emergency there's the Ganges Harbour fast boat. There are not many year-round residents [about 300] but we get a hell of an overload in the summer. I'm glad to see Labour Day come and all the silly little idiots put their toys and playthings away and they go back under their rock in town. That's what I call them—insects. When the sun's nice and bright you'll see them everywhere, but when it's raining they go crawl under a rock."

For those who do stay, finding a means to survive may require inventive or unusual solutions. Oil-drilling was attempted on the island in the 1950s; currently there is an oyster farm near Dave's docking facilities in Boot Cove. In the 1870s and 1880s Japanese immigrants living on Tumbo Island built several charcoal-making pits on Saturna. Now covered with thorny blackberry bushes and salal, these pits are still relatively intact but difficult to find. The charcoal produced there was used by Chinese workers in British Columbia's fish canneries. Cans were hand-soldered at the time and the charcoal was used to heat the soldering irons. According to Dave, the Japanese fished the Fraser River in the summer months and spent the winter making charcoal on Saturna: "The charcoal pits are about twelve to fourteen feet in diameter and the walls built three or four feet into the ground. The pits were lined with rock and the entrance was made in the form of a keyhole. They filled the area with short alder logs and [faster-burning] fir at the mouth. The pit was covered with grassy sod and a big sheet of steel, with a small hole cut in it for a draft, went over that. The fir was lit at the mouth and the slow-burning alder would turn to charcoal. It was taken by wheelbarrow down to barges and shipped over to Steveston where all the big canneries were."

In time, of course, hand-soldering of cans gave way to technological improvements and the Japanese charcoal industry came to an end.

While the Saturna charcoal period came and went fairly quickly, the lighthouse at East Point, which was originally established in 1887, is still

Boot Cove, Saturna Island, ca. 1947.

functional today. Currently it is operated by the Coast Guard, but for most of its lifetime it was tended by individuals contracting with the federal government. Today, a trip to the East Point lighthouse reveals trim, tidy, white and red buildings flanked by a chain-link fence. The buildings overlook the Strait of Georgia and Boundary Pass with views to the east and south of Tsawwassen, Bellingham and the American San Juan Islands. At waterline, the collar of East Point is made up of pockmarked sandstones with peculiar circular depressions produced by uneven "honeycomb" weathering of the sand grain's calcite cement. If you look carefully there are several Indian petroglyphs in the form of fish, carved in relief on the rocks.

For Dave Jack, survival on Saturna meant developing a boat-making business, but along with other residents, he has had to supplement this with other occupations—and a "live and let live" philosophy shared by many islanders. "What do people do to stay alive? They stay out of other people's business. I came here because I had to have a place to build a boat and that sawmill at Winter Cove was very handy. I fished in the summer. We'd haul freight around the islands in the winter. We hauled all the freight to Tumbo Island. They had a caretaker that lived out there and we took food out there twice a year. I logged in the winter, too. Now I'll tell you another story. Ol' Aggie Paul, she used to pull whistle for the high-lead logging shows. Whistle punkin', they called it. Aggie liked to sun herself on this stump she sat on. She had it built up with all these branches so she had a little nest and no one could see her. Her brother said to me, 'Hey, fisher-boy, I dare you to go up there and just push those branches apart and yell *Boo!*' I didn't know she was sunbathin'! I goes up there, opens it up, and she lets out a shriek. She had a big stick and jumped off that stump with nothin' on her top and was after me like you wouldn't believe. And the boys were all yellin', 'Run, fisher-boy, run!' God, she was mad. But you know, it didn't cost much for things in those days. If I wanted a rock cod,

heck, I could get them at high water right in front of the cabin. Just went down with a gas lamp and speared one. And there were clams and oysters and those four-legged things [deer] walking around in the bush. Very handy, and that's the way I lived. There were only a few people on the island at that time. Maybe forty people."

Today, it is not uncommon for people to move to and leave Saturna Island on a whim, but it is not so easy for the island's younger residents who have been raised there. Island living is different, and while its slow, earthy style may be beneficial to them in ways, it is also difficult for many young adults to adjust to the hectic pace and expectations made of them on the mainland. Dave's adopted son, Mike, soft-spoken and just out of high school, is facing this reality and it worries his father.

"There's not much here for the kids, they just have a few things to fool around with. It makes for a lazy kid. They don't want to do anything here. There's a few things for Mike like chopping wood for the stove and I let him go catch fish. But other kids have oil burners in their houses and they don't chop wood. They don't do a damn thing but sit on their bums, smoke cigarettes and talk, and Mike sees them doing that. He could become a fisherman. And he's learning things from me. There's no one else on the island who's doing sand casting of aluminum and brass. I think he could probably do that if he really wanted. When he's about twenty-two or twenty-three he'll probably go off the island and get a job somewhere. It's going to be hard for him when he gets out into the world. I'll give him this place if he'll do something with it."

And what of the future for Mike and other Islanders? If anything, the prospects for employment on Saturna may even be worse. The island is too small for sustainable logging and what few remaining stands of trees are left will probably remain uncut because of citizen pressure and environmental concerns. Tourism is a possibility, but some islanders resist this and Saturna is off the main ferry route, making it difficult for

Dave and Flo Jack (right) during a visit to the East Point Lighthouse. Andy and Kathleen Ritchie, the lightkeepers, are at left.

visitors to get there. Facilities are at a minimum, although a small lodge and restaurant opened recently. For some reason, commercial fishing has never been a big part of economic life on Saturna and Dave feels the resource is in decline anyway.

"I trolled and trolled all last winter for salmon and didn't find many. [In the past] the Fisheries Department thought there was no end to the herring. So they seined this area out in Georgia Strait by Tumbo Island. They seined it and seined it and Flo and I watched this going on. I told the Fisheries Department, 'You know, those herring stay there. They never move. They're always in that one area.' Now there's no herring. Nobody would believe it. I was working with the Fisheries Department on herring statis-

tics for quite a few years. We'd go out and catch a few herring with line and then check the egg count to determine how close they are to spawning. We also wanted to see what fish were travelling with them. You could tell which herring were going to spawn for they have a funny way of coming in. They have a habit of creeping along the bottom and when you catch some of them you'll find that there's a bunch of non-spawners among the spawners. But then Fisheries started allowing the seiners to catch herring with lights. Oh, I tell you, we went down to take a look once and here were little salmon—hundreds and hundreds of them—in the seine net. Brought up with the light. Little flatfish and rock cod brought up thirty fathoms by huge floodlights. Gee, what a shame. That was the decimation of the herring."

In the midst of these economic problems, land values—and property taxes—continue to rise. Property in the Gulf Islands and San Juans is at a premium and increasingly only wealthy Canadians and Americans can afford to live there. Preservationist groups, such as the Gulf Islands Trust, have formed to try and protect the social and environmental integrity of the islands, but Dave worries that many residents will be forced to live elsewhere.

"Well, I think we are going to be priced off these islands and they'll be made into parks. Either that or only the wealthy will be able to live here. Do you know, even the water is expensive here. It costs us over $600 a year for water from the island reservoir. One of our Members of Parliament thinks that as people die the property cannot be given to their heirs. Did the Islanders ever give him trouble over that! He thought the islands should be turned into a park. We have the Island Trust here to protect us, however, and Saturna is far away, too. [Development] may happen, but not for quite a few years."

Though economic sufficiency and growth management are nagging concerns for Islanders, there is much to be said for life on Saturna. In particular, the sense of isolation from the sprawling Vancouver mainland, only a few dozen miles away across the Strait of Georgia, is extraordinary. The evening lights of Vancouver, Tsawwassen and Bellingham—the dome-shaped glow of humanity—is clearly visible from Saturna, but so is the moon and that's about how far away the mainland hustle-bustle feels—at least for now.

Meanwhile, the joking and laughing continue around the kitchen table just inside the orange door at the Jack residence. In most remote environments residents like to poke fun at "outsiders," and this home is no exception. "Did you hear about the time I shot up the Navy? One night Dave Weatherell left a little bush bike, a motorbike, up the road. He was copper-painting his boat. It was just getting dusk and we heard a bunch of young folks shoutin' and hollerin'. It was Navy cadets. They had a pig barbecue going and

Flo Jack ca. early 1970s.

were walking back to their lifeboat to go back out to the ship. We heard them saying, 'How do you start it?' Dave says, 'They're taking my bike!' He started to run after them and I said, 'Don't, I have a better idea.' I gets out the .303, leans out the window and aims it about where the Navy ships were. *Kapow!* We heard them drop the bike and they ran up the road in a cloud of dust. I thought, 'There'll be somebody comin' back.' I went out quietly and three of them were coming back to get the bike. So I went *clink-clunk* with the bolt. There were five officers coming along behind them. Somebody said, 'What's going on here?' I said, 'All you Navy guys got to do is bother people on the island. Steal motorbikes and cause people trouble. C'mon, on your way or you'll get some lead like the other bunch got!' Oh my God, did they go!

"The funny thing about that was old Arthur Ralph—he was about ninety-five—was telling any Navy boat that came in, 'Our Davy Jack shot up your Navy!' It got back to the head office in Esquimalt, and they got the RCMP to investigate. Corporal Rhodes came over and I said, 'Geez, what have I done wrong now?' 'Well, Dave,' he said, 'we heard your still blew up and we came to view the wreckage.' That's what he said. Well, I never sold the stuff or caused any trouble. So finally he says, 'Well, it was the Navy, I have to

*Dave Jack aboard **Island Rover**, 1992.*

file a report on what happened.' Meanwhile, up in the attic I had all our mash and the tops of the bottles and they would go *pop*, making funny little noises letting gas off. And behind the stove was the big keg of beer getting ready. Flo put on a kettle and it started to sing so he couldn't hear that. So anyway, I told them about shooting up the Navy and the cops didn't like those Navy guys and the Corporal started to laugh. That was a good one."

Through all of this I chuckle and laugh with the others while marvelling at the genuine friendliness of Dave and Flo Jack and the pragmatic simplicity of their life. Glancing around an adjacent room, I reflect on the cluttered memorabilia of their half-century on Saturna Island. There are photos of ships, lighthouses and island people. Wall shelves jammed with books, pamphlets and journals, mostly of forest–ocean–ship–fish subject matter. A small, two-horsepower steam engine sits on the floor. An antique spyglass is perched precariously on a window shelf. Feminine knick-knacks neighbour books like *Bull of the Woods*, John Higgins' *Deckhand's Handbook* and, yes, the *Raincoast Chronicles*.

Later, while others are down by the dock, I unearth a yellowing, dog-eared 1964 edition of the Ganges newspaper, the *Gulf Island Driftwood*. In it are the following words:

"Papa John McMann told us this week all about the new boat that Dave Jack has built, 41 feet long with an 11-foot beam in his yard at Boot Cove. She was launched on August 24th, 'christened with real champagne,' and Edna Slater composed the following poem in her honour. You will note the first letter of each line spells out her name: *Saturna Rose*. We think this is just beautiful:

Swift be my hull through the cold salt clud
Alert be my skipper and mate
True be my compass and true be my course
Under God be my fortune and fate
Rich be the harvest I reap from the sea
Nimble my rudder and wheel
Able the hands on engine and gear
Rigid and strong be my keel
Open the heart, my bulwarks and cloves
Sweet be their work and their love
Enduring as oak be their partnership and
 peaceful the seas that they rove."

In the early days, telephone poles were hoisted into hand-dug holes using pike poles and muscle power.

VOICE FROM THE INLET

Don Benson

THE TELEPHONE CAME TO BRITISH Columbia soon after its invention by Alexander Graham Bell in 1876 because it was able to piggyback on bare telegraph wires that had been in use for a decade. The first conversations were transmitted over existing telegraph lines, and BC's first telephone men were experienced telegraphers who understood electricity.

In 1877 Frank Little, a Nanaimo mining engineer, read an article in *Scientific American*, complete with technical descriptions and diagrams, about a marvellous new invention called the "telephone." He gave the article to William Wall, an enterprising young mechanic at the mine, and instructed him to make two "talking boxes." Using copper bands off black powder kegs, borrowed magnets, photographic tintypes and various other odds and ends, Wall haywired together the first pair of commercial telephones used in BC. Electrical power for the talking circuit was provided by batteries he made from old jam jars.

The phones were hooked up to the existing telegraph wire strung between the mine at Wel-

BCTel engineer Cyrus McLean conducted wireless experiments that helped launch Northwest Tel, the world's first radiotelephone company.

lington and colliery wharves at Departure Bay, five miles distant. The principle was almost as primitive as using two tin cans and a taut string, but it worked first try.

As with all of the earliest telephones, one diaphragm served as both transmitter and receiver. The user alternately spoke into the aperture, then held it to his ear to listen. To signal the person at the other end of the line, the user tapped on his telephone with a pencil, and the tapping sound emerged from the other phone.

Early in 1878, Robert McMicking, one of the famous Overlanders of 1862 who had left the Cariboo goldfields and worked his way up to be superintendent of all the government telegraph lines in BC, was offered the agency for the Bell Telephone Company of Canada. In March the first consignment of Bell telephones arrived in Victoria, to be rented out for $20 per year each. For demonstration purposes, McMicking installed one telephone in his telegraph office and another in the editorial rooms of the Victoria *Colonist*, and connected them via the telephone lines.

McMicking set about drumming up business, but was hindered because most people in Victoria perceived the telephone as only a novelty. In the early days of 1880, the first telephone line to give regular communication between two points in Victoria was put into service between Jeffree's clothing store and Pendray's soap factory. But these phones had been purchased in San Francisco. Jolted by the competition, McMicking helped to organize the Victoria & Esquimalt Telephone Company, BC's first telephone company. It opened for business in July, with forty customers hooked up through a switchboard designed by McMicking and built at Albion Iron Works.

The first telephone line on the mainland of British Columbia was strung up at Metlakatla near Prince Rupert in 1880. McMicking leased two Bell telephones to the controversial Anglican missionary William Duncan, and they were shipped north by steamer with a do-it-yourself installation kit.

One old Indian, Walking-On-The-Air, was convinced that Duncan had made a mistake by installing the telephone service, as the devices obviously already spoke English, but would have to be taught the complicated Tsimshian language to be of use.

In 1883 William Weeks and Charles Foster, two American real estate hustlers, went to J.C. "Cariboo Joe" Armstrong for help to finance the New Westminster & Port Moody Telephone

Users of the first "talking boxes" with a single aperture were told: "Don't talk with your ear and listen with your mouth!"

J.C. "Cariboo Joe" Armstrong.

Most of BC's early telephone men were telegraph men who understood electricity, or sailors used to climbing ship's rigging.

Company. A year later Armstrong took over the company for $26 owing on a barrel of glass insulators. Armstrong would eventually help parlay the infant company into the province-wide British Columbia Telephone Company. According to one of New Westminster's first telephone men, George Pittendrigh, "J.C. Armstrong wore a straw hat in summer and winter and was known as 'Cariboo Joe' because he had walked to the Cariboo carrying his blankets and struck it rich. He didn't know much about the mechanical operation of the new telephone system, but he walked around New Westminster carrying a long pole to separate the wires when they got tangled."

At first, Chinese were employed to do all the outside labour for Armstrong. Then one day Pittendrigh decided to lend a hand to some Chinese who were setting a pole near the river. They had lifted the heavy pole, and were about to place the butt in the hole when the noon whistle blew for lunch. The Chinese instantly dropped the pole to the ground. Pittendrigh fell to his knees and suffered a bad back wrench. From that day forward, during his long career in the telephone business, he never again allowed Chinese to be employed.

Before the turn of the century, the Canadian government operated a telephone line on Vancouver Island's rugged West Coast. The fragile eighty-mile line was strung along a section of coast known as the "Graveyard of the Pacific." Many ships, missing the entrance to the Strait of Juan de Fuca in bad weather, were dashed against the reefs and rocks of the exposed coastline.

Signs posted along the beach pointed to shacks the government had erected every ten or fifteen miles. Each shack was supplied with fuel, food, canned milk, blankets, medical kit and a crank telephone. Instructions in several languages explained how to crank the telephone and directed that if there was no response, the wire was to be cut. That would bring the nearest trouble-shooting lineman to their aid.

The shacks were never locked. Fuel and provisions were always replaced, and there is no recorded incidence of theft or vandalism.

In 1898 Dave Logan was hired as a lineman to patrol the uninhabited section of trail between Carmanah Point and Cape Beale. The thankless job paid only $48 a month. Logan often went barefoot on the trail, and travelled with his friendly red dog day and night, repairing line breaks. When asked how he found his way in the dark, he said that he hung onto the red dog's tail. Logan was to maintain the wire in all weather until 1929, when he was nearly seventy.

Today the marvels of modern transportation and telecommunications are often taken for granted, even in isolated places. But early in the century, transportation along British Columbia's coast was catch-as-catch-can and telecommunication between coastal settlements was almost nonexistent.

As soon as telegraph land-lines became a commercial success in the mid-1800s, inventive genius turned to the idea of submarine cables — cables that could be laid on the bottom of a river or ocean to link points separated by water. Numerous experiments to develop submarine cable were conducted, but failed because the insulation surrounding the telegraph wire broke down and leaked. Some success was gained by surrounding the wire with tarred rope or yarn covered with pitch, but only for a limited time. And the idea of threading the wires through leaded pipe worked well in New York Harbour, until the pipe was broken by a freeze-up in the winter of 1846.

The coming of submarine cable might have been delayed indefinitely if a British doctor stationed in Singapore hadn't become curious about a type of whip used in Malaya. The whip was made of gutta percha, a tough pliable material resembling rubber, which eventually proved to be ideal for insulating wire from water.

The first submarine telephone cable laid in British Columbia serviced the salmon canners on Westham Island at the mouth of the Fraser River. Faced with the challenge of getting a line across Canoe Pass, the cannery owners bought a piece of old telegraph cable from the CPR and laid it across the bottom of the passage at slack tide. The line was an instant money-saver. For the first time, the canneries could communicate by phone to control the supply at the various operations and reduce spoilage.

In 1904 a submarine cable was laid between islands in the Gulf of Georgia. When connected to land lines, this would provide the first telephone communication between Vancouver and Victoria. The new line ran from Bellingham to Lummi, Orcas, Shaw and San Juan Islands, following the general route of the original Western Union telegraph line maintained by Robert McMicking four decades earlier.

The twin-screw steamer *Rapid Transit* was used for laying the cable. George McCartney, superintendent of construction for BCTel, handled the brake machine. The little steamer had trouble bucking the current between the San Juan Islands and Vancouver Island. Because it could not hold a straight course, a lot of cable was wasted.

W.T. Henley, the English cable manufacturing company, sent out a team of installation specialists. McCartney recalled: "Special care was taken of the splicer. He did nothing but make the splice, while his assistants did everything else. The object was to keep his hands soft, so that he could work the pliable gutta percha closely about the conductors. That a special man like this should be brought from London for work which took only a few hours shows to what care the manufacturers went to see that the work was well done."

After the submarine cable was laid, McCartney and his gang spent twelve days splicing up the shore ends and testing the circuits. The submarine cable had cost about $7,000 a mile, but it cost twice that amount to replace one foot of it a couple of months later. The strong rushing tides had pushed the cable back and forth across a sharp reef, wearing a hole through the protective sheathing.

By 1929 there were six toll circuits linking

BCTel's cableship, the **Brico**.

Vancouver to Vancouver Island at Nanaimo. The circuits were carried by submarine cable from the mainland to Newcastle Island in Nanaimo harbour. The remaining few hundred yards of water were crossed by special bare steel wires strung on 100-foot-high poles.

Early one winter night the mast of a tall ship passing underneath struck the wires. Being made of steel, they didn't break, but became twisted together, shorting out and totally interrupting phone service on the Island. Nanaimo plant chief Leo Griggs and his crew worked all night to clear the trouble. First a lineman climbed one of the high poles and put a sliding ring around one of the wires. Then he hauled up the end of a long rope coiled in a rowboat below and attached it to the ring. The boat's crew then rowed along the length of the wires, pulling the ring after them. When the ring jammed at the point where the wires were tangled, the crew played out the rope until they reached the opposite shore. From firm ground they tugged hard on the rope until the ring came free, separating the wire it was riding on

from the others. They repeated the process in the opposite direction, back and forth, until all the lines were clear. Service was restored by six the next morning.

After nearly a decade as BCTel's cable-laying vessel, the wooden-hulled *Iwalani* was replaced by the steel-hulled *Brico* in 1930. Built in Seattle in 1908 for deep-sea halibut fishing, the vessel was originally called the *Chicago* and was renamed the *Brico* by BCTel as an abbreviation of British Columbia Telephone Company.

At a Vancouver shipyard the cable-laying machinery and deckhouse were transferred from the *Iwalani* to the new vessel, and a wheelhouse was placed on top of the deckhouse, assuring good visibility for navigation. The *Brico*'s hold accommodated half again as much cable as that of the *Iwalani*. She had bunks for thirty-three men, twenty-four in the forward hold, six in three compartments on the main deck aft, and three next to the galley aft, for the cook and flunkies.

As a cableship, the *Brico* did not operate under her own power, but was towed and guided

*In order to lay twelve miles of cable across the gulf, telephone men had to walk as far as sixteen miles around the hold of the **Brico**.*

by a pair of tugs. The captain, Bill Grisenthwaite, skippered the *Brico* on every single run from her maiden voyage to her final voyage thirty-two years later, and retired from the company after the *Brico* was decommissioned in 1962.

The *Brico* traveled 25,000 miles—the distance around the world at the equator—for BCTel. The last of the cable-laying vessels in BC waters, she was eventually converted for use as a restaurant at Fanny Bay on the east coast of Vancouver Island.

In 1917 BCTel president William Farrell established Oaks Point Camp exclusively for operators at Buccaneer Bay on Thormanby Island, forty miles north of Vancouver. Sleeping tents were set up facing out across the water in the shadow of the large trees. The operators enjoyed rowing, fishing, hiking and playing tennis on a wooden court. After dark they gathered around a large bonfire on the beach to swap stories and sing songs. The camp was intended to be a unisex summer resort for the hundreds of female telephone operators. But to Farrell's disappointment, the operators preferred shopping in Seattle to vacationing on a remote island away from their gentleman friends. Eventually, couples were allowed to vacation at Oaks Point, but as that wasn't Farrell's original intent, the property was sold.

In 1924 three government technicians arrived at Gibsons to experiment with the feasibility of connecting the Sunshine Coast telephone network to Vancouver using the existing telegraph cable. Mrs. Lou Winn, who was hired as the first telephone operator at Gibsons, recalled that the telegraph technicians managed to make the appropriate electrical connections after a couple of days, but all they knew about telephones was that

BCTel operators at Oak Points camp during the summer of 1918.

you cranked the handle to get someone's attention, and lifted the receiver off the switch hook to talk. And that was all the instructions she was given for a job that lasted more than thirty years.

As telegraph transmission continued to be the government's priority during business hours, telephone calls to Vancouver were limited to early morning and evening hours for the first three years. The first telephone exchange was in the dining room of the Winns' home. Every time a call was made, every bell on every telephone would ring. The bells tinkled around the clock. Subscribers soon knew all the ring codes and who was being called, and even came to recognize who was placing the call by the way the caller turned the crank on the generator.

In those days before electronic home entertainment, people used to amuse themselves by listening in on calls—especially long distance conversations. Sometimes there were so many listeners that the transmission level fell, and the callers had to shout to be heard, or ask the eavesdroppers to get off the line. There was no such thing as "personal" calls because there was absolutely no privacy.

If any one man gave voice to the coast, it

was Cyrus Hale McLean. Born on Prince Edward Island in 1898, Cyrus McLean moved to Vancouver with his family at the age of seven. In 1914 he started with BCTel at the old headquarters on Yukon Street as a $25-a-month messenger boy. By the age of twenty-two he had worked his way up to being the New Westminster wire chief. He then studied electrical engineering at night school to become BCTel's first transmission engineer.

In 1929, McLean was put in charge of a series of radiotelephone experiments, designed to overcome the problems associated with providing service to the coastal inlets. For two years McLean travelled up and down the coast on the motor launch *Belmont* with a transmitter and receiver on board. A typical day started before dawn and ended about eight at night when they dropped anchor in some handy cove. McLean recalls: "At isolated ports like Klemtu or Anyox we'd invite local businessmen to use our radio facilities to talk to their family and friends in Vancouver. For some of them, who had been cut off from voice contact with the outside world for a long time, it was an emotional experience. Some had tears in their eyes."

After pioneering radiotelephone on British

*A rented motor yacht, the **Belmont**, was fitted out with special high masts for transmitting and receiving experimental radiotelephone calls.*

Columbia's coast, McLean became radio communications consultant for BCTel's parent company GTE, and its subsidiaries in Colombia, Venezuela, the Dominican Republic, Haiti and the Philippines. He took over as president of BCTel in 1958.

In 1971, fifty-seven years after he delivered his first message by bicycle for BCTel, Cyrus McLean stepped down as chairman of the board. Less than a century after Bell patented the telephone, Marshal McLuhan noted: "The telephone began as a novelty, became a necessity, and now is regarded as an absolute right." On Canada's West Coast that right was hard won. Stringing bare iron wires through British Columbia's dense rain forests and along her rough-chiselled coastline was one of the most adventurous, technically difficult telecommunications projects undertaken anywhere in the world.

Adam Waldie, age 21, Rivers Inlet; 1947.

SUMMER INTERN AT BELLA BELLA 1947

Adam C. Waldie

THE CANADIAN COAST GUARD CUTTER *George E. Darby*, agent of so many dramatic maritime rescues, is a fitting symbol of the life and works of the man for whom it is named. Dr. George Elias Darby was the consummate physician, an ordained minister of the Methodist Church, a justice of the peace and a small-time researcher into the anthropology and ethnology of the north-central BC coast.

His Canadian parents had left their upstate New York home, where his father was a success-ful veterinarian, to move to Vancouver about 1908. There the senior Darby sold real estate, and he and his family were active in the building of the Crosby Memorial Methodist Church, now rebuilt as Kitsilano United Church. In the meantime, George entered the University of Toronto, where he was an excellent student, graduating with the silver medal in medicine. During his student years he became very moved by the adventures and appeals of the Methodist missionaries home on furlough, so it was not

Dr. George Elias Darby, 1889-1962.

surprising that while on summer holiday he responded to an urgent request to assist the medical missionary at Bella Bella and Rivers Inlet whose partner had died suddenly of a strep throat.

Darby had spent barely a week being oriented into frontier medicine when the doctor and his wife left suddenly on an hour's notice and caught the steamer for Vancouver. This left Darby, working on a temporary licence, as the sole medical resource for Bella Bella, Klemtu, Namu and Rivers Inlet with thousands of native people and seasonal workers—fishermen, loggers and cannery workers—dependent on him.

On graduation two years later, Darby interned at the Vancouver General Hospital, then went east to marry his fiancee, Edna Matthews, who was also a student at the University of Toronto and an accomplished tennis player. After a leisurely honeymoon in New York State and in the Canadian West, they took up residence in Bella Bella. The same month, World War One was declared.

Darby agonized whether to join the army or to stay to serve the people of the coast. He chose the latter and almost immediately was caught up in the hectic life of providing medical care, building a new hospital, assisting with the design and installation of a water supply and the construction of the first wharf. Before the hospital was completed, the Spanish flu of 1919 decimated the village, and no sooner had the dock been built than it was demolished by a ship trying to tie up in a violent windstorm.

At a special convocation of the Columbia Theological College of the BC Methodist synod in 1919, Dr. George Darby was ordained as a minister of the gospel. His biographer, Reverend Hugh McKerville, leaves little doubt that Darby's formal theological training was rudimentary to say the least, and the ordination was more in the nature of an honorary appointment. As a justice of the peace, his quasi-judicial functions were said to be equally informal; people appearing before him tended to receive counselling or perhaps a prayer, and any sentencing was left to a higher court.

Darby's study of the link of the coast natives with the Mongolian people across the Bering Sea followed a more disciplined course and was published in the journal of the Royal College of Anthropology. For this work he received an Honorary Fellowship in the Royal College of Anthropology in 1931. He used to speak to me of visits from Franz Boas, the great German ethnologist and linguist who, he said, could take down a conversation in a phonetic shorthand and repeat it back so that the natives could understand it, though he did not comprehend a single word himself.

Darby never learned the Bella Bella language, but he was a master of Chinook, the *lingua franca* of traders, missionaries and natives in the Northwest. I once heard him preach a sermon in Chinook because so many of the old people could not understand English. Today the Chinook jargon is extinct except for a few words which have been absorbed into our own language: skookum, chuck, mug-up (muck-a-muck) and tillacum.

The legend of Dr. Darby expanded for nearly half a century. Anyone who travelled the north-central coast knew his reputation, and he was one of the brightest stars in the galaxy of the Home Mission Board of the Methodist Church (which became the United Church of Canada after 1926). The names of men such as Thomas Crosby, the great explorer-missionary of the latter half of the nineteenth century, Dr. R.W. Large of Bella Bella, Port Simpson and Prince Rupert, and Dr. Horace Wrinch of Hazelton, became household words to the church people of eastern Canada as they received and supported the deputation efforts of the missionaries on furlough. Like his predecessors, Darby did not isolate himself in his hospital-kingdom. He travelled with the native people on their migrations to Goose Banks, Milbanke Sound, and especially in Namu and Rivers Inlet for the annual salmon runs. As a capable physician and a fearless man of God, Darby developed a well-earned reputation for his medical skills and his practical Christianity.

A brass band playing at a wedding in Bella Bella, 1947.

I do not remember how I, a Baptist at the time, first heard of this frontier physician, or knew that he took a medical student every year as a summer assistant. Regardless, in June 1947, I applied for and got the job, and travelled north on the Union steamship S.S. *Catalla*, stopping in at many camps and hamlets en route. As I debarked at Bella Bella, one of the hospital staff said, "Dr. Darby wants you in the operating room right away." Having rarely if ever been in an operating room before, I wondered what could be happening. I walked in, scrubbed, put on the obligatory cap, mask and gown and finally met Dr. Darby, who was standing at the operating table about to drain a huge breast abscess. He thrust a scalpel into my hand and said, "Cut here along the crease between the breast and the chest wall." Several

ounces of foul-smelling, creamy pus oozed out of the incision. He instructed me to make another cut along the top of the breast and insert a large, soft rubber drain between the mass of breast tissue and the chest wall itself. Had I known anything at all about the surgical drainage of a breast abscess I might not have appeared to be so inept, but it was all very new to me at the time.

That same evening during dinner we were called upstairs to the maternity ward, where a young lady was having a baby so quickly they didn't have time to move her into the caseroom. I was given a pair of gloves to slip on quickly and delivered the baby with Darby standing by. I didn't have to do much but stay out of the way while nature took its course, but I quickly learned the reason for the somewhat earthy term "baby catching." It was my first delivery with about twelve hundred more to come in the next forty years.

The village of Bella Bella at that time was about sixty years old. Five or six smaller settlements from around the Llama Passage and Milbanke Sound areas had come together before the turn of the century for purposes of school, church and medical care, provided in this case by the Methodists. The original settlement was located on Campbell Island near the abandoned Hudson's Bay Company Fort McLoughlin, but about 1890 it was moved a mile or so north to its present site. A long, elevated boardwalk over the muskeg served as a main street, with the houses built on lateral extensions of the main thoroughfare. A modest white church in the late-nineteenth-century Methodist style was the centre for worship, christenings, marriages and funerals. A large, reusable supply of paper flowers provided the decorations for all occasions. While there was usually a minister in residence, there often was a vacancy, and Dr. Darby frequently officiated at Sunday services and prayer meetings. He was not an eloquent speaker and always preached in a combination of Chinook and English. In the summer of 1947 the supply minister was a Reverend Mr. Johnson who had been the principal of a boys' school on the prairies. His heavy cataract spectacles made him look a little frail, though he was anything but. He would disappear into the village early in the morning and not reappear until late at night. While his vocation was the ministry, his avocation, even passion, was drama. He could recite the plays of Shakespeare for hours on end. One of his sons, Al Johnson, became president of the CBC. The other, Dr. T. Carman Johnson, is a well-known physician in West Vancouver.

On several occasions I made house calls with Dr. Darby, visiting some of the older bedridden people in the village. One was a cancer patient in some pain; the doctor asked for a teaspoon, dropped a morphine tablet in it with a little water, brought it to a boil in the flame of a coal-oil lamp, took it up in a glass syringe and administered it as a hypodermic injection. It would be another twenty years before plastic disposable syringes became available and a further fifteen years before liquid morphine came into common use.

Dr. Darby was a bit disappointed that I was only a third-year student from the new four-year course; he was used to having help with a little more experience. Nevertheless, he bit his lip and with remarkable patience set about teaching me the rudiments of doing blood counts, sedimentation rates, urinalyses, x-rays and minor surgery. Within the first twenty-four hours he handed me a green textbook with the title *EXODONTIA* in large gold capitals. "Read this from cover to cover," he said, "and know everything that is in it." With no dentist between Powell River and Prince Rupert, pulling abscessed and painful teeth was an everyday task for doctors at the time. "Never leave a root in. If it breaks off, go after it with an elevator." He had no truck with timidity. "If you can't get a tooth out, don't be afraid to cut away some of the alveolar ridge with bone rongeurs; you can always suture the flap." His local anaesthetics were meticulous and he expected ours to be the same, including mandibular blocks. Later, on my rounds of the various camps and canneries at Rivers Inlet, I carried two black bags: one contained the blood pressure cuff, stethoscope and a few basic medications, the other an elaborate set of dental instruments. Frequently a fisherman would track me down complaining of a throbbing tooth and I would have to sit him on the closest box or fence and do a dental extraction then and there.

Productive coughs were common, and tuberculosis always had to be excluded. There were many cases of erysipeloid, a low-grade inflammation of the skin caused by puncture wounds from fish teeth. It was extremely resistant to treatment until the advent of sulfa drugs and later antibiotics. The summer of 1947 was the first time penicillin became available in non-military hospitals, but supplies were limited. It had to be given every three hours by injection, though we were beginning to combine it with peanut oil to prolong the absorption.

Fishermen suffered a great number of broken ribs from falling on the slippery decks. They would tough out the pain for several days, then come in to have their ribs strapped until the pain peaked out on the eighth day. Running ears were endemic; chronic tonsillitis with foul running noses and swollen lymph glands were almost the norm. The larger neck swellings were often tuberculosis glands and sooner or later formed draining sinuses; these patients had to go to the city or to one of the TB sanitaria for surgical treatment.

Tuberculous meningitis was not uncommon and always fatal. One of my first lessons in the cultural nuances of medicine occurred directly as a result of a case of this disease in a three-year-old boy from Kitimat, a two-day trip up coast by small boat. The lad had been languishing in the hospital for a couple of weeks and one morning, when Dr. Darby had just left on a five-day trip, the mother came to me and asked if there was any hope her boy might live. "Unfortunately," I said, "there are no recorded cases of survival." Then she asked if they might take him back home. There was no one to appeal to for an opinion so I took it on myself to say they could, and he died en route. When Dr. Darby returned he said to me, "You will never know how grateful those people will be to you. If the child had died here the Bella Bella people would have taken them in and provided a funeral and funeral feast and seen them through the occasion. But according to the very strong imperative of the native custom, the Kitimat people would have had a very serious obligation to invite the Bella Bellas back to their home to provide a much larger celebration than the original one. They would have been broke for a year paying back all the debts incurred to stage such a feast."

It is said that doctors as a group suffer from thanatophobia, or fear of death. If this is true it is no wonder; death still occurs so unpredictably and almost never when we think it will. Having learned many times never to venture a guess when it will happen, I still get caught out occasionally despite myself. The first experience occurred during my early days at Bella Bella. A beautiful native girl of twelve or fourteen had come in with multiple spontaneous bruises and bleeding from every orifice of her body. Dr. Darby had done the blood tests and confirmed she had an absence of blood platelets which are required for clotting. The condition is well known, despite its long name, as idiopathic thrombocytopenic purpura, or simply Werlhof's disease. A patient with a less fulminant case might have been saved by removal of the spleen, but this was out of the question.

Suddenly the girl became unconscious. The mother asked me how long it would be. Gravely I checked the pulse, temperature, breathing and blood pressure, all normal, and announced it would be a day or two. A few minutes later I came by and the mother was sobbing out, "Goodbye, goodbye, goodbye." I put on my best professional manner and said, "It will be some time yet." But the mother knew better. "No," she sobbed, "cold right up to the elbows now." In half an hour the girl was dead. Mother had obviously sat in on a good many more deathbed vigils than I had.

While he had been an excellent student, Darby was a born tinkerer and was completely devoid of any sense of time, at least when I knew him. He could fix anything, from the power plant to the boat engine to the x-ray machine, although he admitted he was no carpenter. Shortly before I arrived the new Spilsbury–Hepburn short-wave radio had been installed, a giant leap forward in coastal communications. Periodically it would have a malfunction and Dr. Darby would fiddle with it day and night until he got it going.

He was meticulous in the use of x-ray equipment. Every exposure was listed in a huge ledger, listing the part or area, KVP, time, distance and other selected adjustments. Long before the days of automated processors, the developer and the fixer were always kept at the proper temperature and the solutions fresh. If a film was not perfect

M.V. **William Pierce** *in front of the hospital at Bella Bella, 1947.*

it was repeated. This perfectionist approach was part of his dedication to doing consultant quality work in the treatment of tuberculosis. On one of his sabbaticals he spent some months in England learning the state-of-the-art techniques of artificial pneumothorax, one of the best treatments at the time for pulmonary tuberculosis. It consisted of weekly injections of air into the pleural cavity in order to collapse the underlying lining and put it to rest so the cavity would heal.

One of my duties as a summer intern was to carry the TB cases down from the solarium on the second floor, since there was no elevator, and to x-ray the chest, inject the air and carry the patients back upstairs. Predictably, on my return to Edmonton in the fall I developed a large primary tubercle, or Ghon complex, in my left lung as a result of this overwhelming exposure to open tuberculosis cases. This stage of the disease is usually quite benign but startling to see on the chest films; it heals in a few months, leaving a calcified scar and usually a degree of immunity. The reinfection type, on the other hand, is much more serious, and prior to antituberculosis drugs it often went on to cavity formation, hemorrhage and, not infrequently, death.

Venereal disease was a big worry in the 1940s, but we saw little of it up coast. A local chief from the Rivers Inlet area came in with his wife, both suffering from large ulcers in the mid-shin area. Silver nitrate was said to be a good treatment for ulcers, so I was busy touching them up with this substance when Dr. Darby passed by, tapped me on the shoulder and said, "Save your time, Adam, those are luetic gummata" (third-stage syphilitic lesions in the skin). Even then they were medical museum pieces, and the only ones I have ever seen to this day. Later at Rivers Inlet the nurse and I watched a young deckhand from the federal survey ship, the *William J. Stewart*, walk up the path from the dock to the hospital. "He's got VD," she said. Incredulous, I asked her how she could tell. "Just watch him looking around to see if anyone is staring at him," she replied. Sure enough, he had a classic case of gonorrhea. At that time we had to fill out a long questionnaire for epidemiological details. Everything went well until we came to the question of where exposure took place. At this point the young man stammered and turned red in acute embarrassment. "On the water tower at Namu," he replied. Of course I had to laugh, but he blurted out: "It was the only dry place there was!"

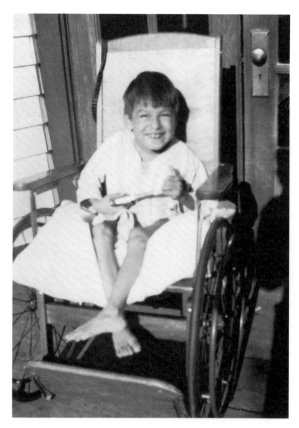

Vincent Hunt, six years old, suffered from fragilitas ossium, or brittle bone disease. By this age he had sustained over fifty fractures, most of which had been spontaneous. At the time of this picture he had broken his wrist peeling an orange.

One morning after taking a message on the radiotelephone, Dr. Darby announced that Dr. Ted Whiting wanted me to go to Bella Coola, ninety miles east, to cover for him while he made his annual trip by horseback to the interior to visit the natives of Ulgatcho and Anahim Lake. As a third-year student I protested that I was not qualified to hold down a twenty-bed hospital in a community of eight hundred people with no telephones and only one boat a week.

"What's the matter?" he asked. "Are you scared?"

"Yes," I said. "But if that's the way you feel about it, I'll go."

The *Black Hawk*, the BC Packers speedboat, took me to Namu, twenty-five miles away, and after overnighting in the first-aid office I caught the S.S. *Catala* to Bella Coola, arriving after dark. Exploring the next morning, I found

a small native village with houses here and there in the forest, and a small community of whites nearby. Each settlement had its own church. Cliff Kopas's general store was in a low cottage and on entering I found a small stock of groceries, clothing and hardware and a huge stock of books. He was later to publish the definitive book *Bella Coola* and an account of his honeymoon called *Packhorses to the Pacific*. Numerous small, painted grave boxes were visible in the nearby trees, apparently preserved from disintegration in the wet forest by being stored on branches off the ground.

The old x-ray machine had open-lead wiring, and the diesel generator had to run for half an hour to charge its batteries enough for a couple of exposures. The operating room, caseroom and wards were on the second floor, with kitchens, laundry, pharmacy and clinic offices on the ground level. Fortunately there were no serious cases to tax my limited training and experience, but there were two obstetric deliveries, a fractured collarbone, a paracentesis (drainage) of an abdomen for accumulated fluid from syphilitic heart disease, and a girl with a severe septic throat which did not respond to sulfa drugs and used up my small supply of penicillin. A native boy appeared with fourteen feet of tapeworm (diphyllobothrium latum) wound around a stick of kindling.

It was many years later, on reading McKerville's biography, that I realized Darby was getting back his own by sending me to Bella Coola. He had been through a similar experience forty years before. Certainly as a teacher he had a unique way of giving medical students unlimited opportunity to establish their confidence with a minimum of direction and supervision. But it was a two-way street: he depended on his summer interns to keep him abreast of the current teachings in the medical schools.

Even in the days before Air Sea Rescue or the Provincial Emergency Service with its air ambulances, it is interesting to realize how seldom we used the operating room in the three months of my summer internship. There was the drainage of the breast abscess on my first day. Dr. Darby did a hernia repair for a fisherman and made no apology for having a textbook beside the operating table to refresh his memory of the surgical anatomy of the inguinal canal. There was one tonsillectomy in which he used an old-fashioned Sleuter, or guillotine, which looked for all the world like one of those gadgets used for cutting off the ends of cigars. On the other hand, Dr. Darby used an endotracheal tube which was very new at the time but a *sine qua non* today.

On the first day I was left alone when Dr. Darby made his annual trip to Kitimat, I had to open a huge abscess in the palm of a ten-year-old boy who had been brought in on an overnight trip from Smith Inlet, eighty miles south. By giving a barbiturate capsule rectally we were able to get by with a minimum of open-drop ether anaesthetic, and the boy's rapid recovery after adequate surgical drainage was almost miraculous.

The little summer hospital at Brunswick on Rivers Inlet was more or less completely equipped for emergency work, but I can recall that it was used only once in the six or eight weeks we were there. One of the Schuetze boys whom I had met at Bella Coola the previous week came in off a seiner with acute appendicitis. There was no elevator and the operating room was on the third level in order to take advantage of the light from a skylight in that wet, grey climate, so the patient had to walk up. Dr. Darby gave him a spinal anaesthetic and took out a gangrenous appendix. The biggest difficulty was positioning the operating table so that rain from the leaky skylight would not fall on the incision area. Otherwise, Danny made a rapid recovery and was discharged in two days rather than the conventional five.

For sheer life-and-death drama we had just one case that summer, and we lost the gamble. While I was away at Bella Coola, Dr. Darby and the staff made the annual migration to Rivers Inlet, leaving behind a skeleton crew with Dr. Murray Fraser, who had just done a very busy surgical internship in Regina. He had been on his own for a couple of days when a young lady was admitted after a two-day boat trip from Kitimat. She had a bowel obstruction of several days' duration and was very seriously ill. Her chances

Egg Island lighthouse, 1947.

of survival without operation were zero, and only slightly better if Murray operated. He did his best to hydrate her and to make a stab at restoring some electrolytes, but there was no lab service available except for basic blood counts. Nurse Flora Moffat gave a very smooth open-drop ether anaesthetic, but the situation was desperate. To shorten the operating time, Murray used a Murphy button—like a dome fastener, even then a museum piece—to join the two pieces of the intestine. The patient died soon after leaving the operating table, but we had to wait a couple of days for the steamer to take the body to Kitimat. The family purchased a coffin for eighty dollars from the BC Packers store at old Bella Bella, near the RCAF base at Shearwater. When the *Catalla* arrived we loaded the coffin on the open back of the hospital's old Model T Ford and drove the couple of blocks to the wharf. As the coffin was placed on the pallet board, three crew members stood on each side, seamen's caps in hand, and

*Lighthouse tender, M.V. **Alberni**, at Namu.*

stood to attention while the winch hauled it up to the deck for the long trip home to Kitimat.

Harold Malm of Sointula was the camp boss for the Canadian Fishing Company at Margaret Bay, south of Rivers Inlet. He had just taken possession of a high-speed boat called the *Ripon Point*, equipped with short-wave radios so he could direct his fishermen to hot fishing areas. One evening toward the end of summer a fish packer came into Bella Bella with two stretcher cases. Harold had just gassed up his boat at Duncanby, near Goose Bay, and when he pressed the starter switch there was a tremendous explosion. He was blown clear through a gaping hole in his cabin roof. Landing on the dock feet first, he broke both his ankles. His crewman casting off the stern line was luckier; he merely ended up in the water across the floats, with minor burns.

It was the custom of the Darbys at the end of every summer to visit the lighthouse keeper at Egg Island at the mouth of Rivers Inlet, taking a few of the younger staff on the old *Edward V. White* and making it an overnight trip, sleeping on board. We arrived late in the evening and dropped the anchor chain close to shore but very deep. A few yards away was a large white cross in memory of two keepers who went fishing one night years before but never returned. In the morning we went ashore and climbed several hundred stairs to the top of the island, then walked along a path and crossed a small footbridge over a ravine to reach the light. We were greeted by an elderly keeper with a long walrus moustache who kindly showed us the ancient machinery which operated the foghorn. A turn-of-the-century Fairbanks–Morse kerosene engine with a long drive belt operated a compressor. He said that running it all morning provided just enough air in the large low-pressure tank to give about a dozen burps on the foghorn.

The lady of the light was something else. She somehow made us a breakfast from her stock of canned goods, then commanded us all to go back to the boat because she had to see the doctor.

Dr. Darby insisted that I accompany him to her boudoir on the second storey of the light, looking out over the shelving reef a couple of hundred feet below. There emerged a crescendo of complaints that is hard to believe in this day and age. They had not seen a single human being for over a year. Their last mail and supplies had been delivered by breeches buoy from the lighthouse tender *Alberni* at Christmas time, eight months earlier. A gale and tidal wave had smashed her second-storey bedroom window, putting two feet of water in her boudoir. Alf had not talked to her for six months. And finally, in utter desperation, she sobbed out, "And doctors, you might as well know it, but Alf and I ain't married."

Dr. Darby promised to write to the DOT verifying the couple would have to break their contract on medical grounds. Six weeks later the *Alberni* carried the keepers to Bella Bella, where it is said the lady stormed across the dock and onto the *Catalla* without even turning to say goodbye to Alf.

One year later a hurricane carried Egg Island lighthouse into the sea. When the tender crew arrived a week later they found the new keeper, his wife and their young son still alive but very ill from thirst, hunger and hypothermia. The man and his son recovered but the wife suffered a permanent nervous breakdown. Quite by chance, while covering for another doctor, I attended her for her last illness in 1976, when she died in the Vancouver General Hospital.

A generation has come and gone since the Darby era ended on the north-central coast, leaving few memories beyond a well-earned reputation and some place names on the nautical charts in the Rivers Inlet area. Though it did not have the wide publicity of the Grenfell Mission in

Keeper of the light at Egg Island, 1947.

Newfoundland and Labrador, it is likely that the Methodist and United Church provided much more state-of-the-art medical services for the times and touched the lives of a good many more people.

Society in general, and professional anthropologists in particular, are questioning the wisdom of the missionaries at the turn of the century in destroying the fabric of the native culture in their zeal to spread the Christian gospel. Whatever the answer, it seems fair to speculate that Bella Bella, now called Waglisla, would not be the thriving native community it is today had not Dr. Darby and others laboured there so long to bridge the gap between the old ways and the new.

PAUL BUNYAN

The Greatest Logger Who Ever Fed a Salesman to a Dog

Tom Henry

PAUL BUNYAN WAS IN BC, THAT much we can prove. For evidence there is the Inside Passage, the Gulf Islands, Mt. Baker and canned meat.

When he was here is more a matter of speculation, although we know it was sometime between the Winter of the Blue Snow (when it got so cold words froze) and the Spring that the Rains Came Up from China (when so many of his crew were carried away by the Big Fog). We also know that his stay here was tragic, and not only because at the Pacific's edge he saw the end of the continent's big timber. For it was here, in a logging camp just north of Vancouver, that Paul's beloved companion Babe the Blue Ox died.

According to old-timers who worked with him, Paul Bunyan was the greatest of loggers. A half-French Canadian, half American, half Scottish son of an eastern woodsman, he was so big that he could cut down trees with a single swipe of his double-bladed axe and comb his beard with a pine tree. He loved cutting trees and hated salesmen and lawyers, who he fed to his pet moosehound, Elmer.

Paul's companion in the woods was Babe, an enormous ox with a horn spread of (depending on the account) 42 axe handles and one plug of Star tobacco, or 42 axe handles and two plugs of Star tobacco. Babe's feet were so big an iron mine had to be opened each time he was shod and he ate so much that he produced 160 feet of manure every night. When Paul was walking behind Babe he often used binoculars to see what the front of the animal was doing.

Paul and Babe started logging on the east coast, and they and their crews had some strange adventures, including an encounter with a river that flowed in circles and a popcorn storm. (Thinking the popcorn was snow, some of Paul's dumber loggers almost froze to death.) On another occasion, in Iowa, some of Paul's crew were struck with a terrible urge to write poetry, and Paul had to kick their heads with his caulk boots until they recanted. (Hence the lack of logging poetry today.)

But it was the Pacific coast where Paul faced his biggest challenges. He originally came west because Babe was ill and his bookkeeper, Johnny Inkslinger, had prescribed milk of the western whale as a cure. The milking turned out to be a fiasco (someone kicked over the pail), but by that time Paul had had a look at the region's first-growth firs and cedars and decided to stay.

The timber in those days really was big, and it often took five or six men looking eight hours to see to the top of a single tree. Occasionally fallers would die of old age before they finished making a cut and the next generation would have

to finish it off.

Paul's West Coast camp, in the Skagit Valley, was the biggest in the world. There were a thousand bunkhouses, each so high that the men in the upper tiers parachuted to the floor each morning. The cookhouse covered so many acres that the crew were given "starter" meals when they first went in so they could make it to the tables. Meals were organized by a cook who rode

around the kitchen on a motorcycle and they were cooked on a 25-block-long griddle greased by Swedish figure skaters with hams tied to their feet. It took flunkies wearing roller skates a full day to go around just one table.

Not long after Paul started logging on the coast, a group of Seattle businessmen came to him with an offer. They would pay him $5 million if he would dig a deep-sea port for the city. (Vancouver Island was part of the mainland at the time.) Paul went north and dragged a glacier back, thus creating the Inside Passage, and used it to dig the Puget Sound. When the businessmen tried to skip on payment (they wanted waves; Paul said they weren't in the contract), Paul picked up a shovel and started refilling the new waterway. The suits paid up, pronto, but the mounds remain. They are the Gulf and San Juan Islands.

The waters of the newly created Puget Sound and Georgia Strait were fine for shipping, but too cold for Paul's men to wash their clothes. So Paul kicked out the Strait of Juan de Fuca, swam a few circles in the Pacific and got the El Nino going. His men washed their clothes in the warm current for years, until other nations started complaining about all the salt and foam and they had to stop.

The Puget Sound excavation contract completed, Paul finally got back to doing what he loved best—logging. But according to old-timers, Babe never did take to life on the coast. (One fellow said Babe was nauseated by the pink umbrellas which were in fashion here at the time.) Babe spent most days tethered with an anchor chain to Mt. Baker, which at that time was in central Washington. One day Babe caught whiff of some pancakes cooking up Vancouver way, and being a sucker for food, started straining. The chain was strong enough but the mountain wasn't. It pulled loose and Babe dragged it all the way to the border before it broke away.

Babe found the pancakes in a camp near the end of Burrard Inlet. Breakfast was just being served, and in two and a half swallows he devoured four platters of pancakes (each four feet high), a table, the cook, the pancake flipper and the woodstove, which had just been stoked with dry spruce. Then he let out a snort, a bellow, and keeled over.

Someone sent for Paul, and the yarding crew tried to drag the stove out with a steam donkey. But it was too late. By the time Paul arrived, Babe the Blue Ox was dead.

What happened after this is a matter of some contention. Some old-timers say that Paul, being a decent sort, buried Babe by the ocean. The grave is called the Olympics. But others contend that Paul was first and foremost an entrepreneur, and that after Babe's carcass had cooked through Paul had him canned and sold to stores. (A corner store in Lake Cowichan apparently still has some of the original stock.)

Paul's immediate fate is also uncertain; he may have gone handlogging in Rivers Inlet, or he may have drifted into one of the infamous Cordova Street beer parlours, where he still languishes. But one thing all legends about him do have in common is that Paul Bunyan was the greatest logger who ever fed a salesman to a dog.

TWENTY-FOUR COLONELS _on the_ WEST ARM ROAD

◆

SHAWNIGAN LAKE _in the_ 1920s

Joan Mason Hurley

OF RECENT YEARS IT HAS BECOME the custom to belittle the "Brits"—those eccentric characters, ex-Army, ex-Navy, definitely British public school, who in the early years of the century when the map was mostly pink, emigrated to this West Coast of ours, thriving vigorously in Qualicum and Duncan, Saltspring Island and the Cowichan Valley, founding private schools, building libraries, constructing community halls—giving the place much of its flavour. Now they are gone and mostly forgotten,

except by a few of us survivors who remember that era with affection.

My husband, Denis Mason Hurley, who came as a boy to live at Shawnigan Lake about 1920, always claimed that in those days there were twenty-four colonels on the West Arm Road. This so-called road was a narrow gravel track, dust in summer, mud and deep snow in winter, which wound for three or four miles out of the village of Shawnigan through the forest along the west arm of the lake.

The colonels were mostly ex-Indian army, or old China hands—Denis's father was one of the latter—all retired in early middle age, with pensions and a little capital but not very much more, not enough to live in the style to which they aspired back "home," but enough to do their sterling best to emulate that style in this remote outpost of Empire. Their years abroad soldiering in the hills and plains of India, or conducting trade in the great cities of Shanghai or Hong Kong, had not fitted them to conform to the constrictions of life in Cheltenham or Brighton—but it hadn't prepared them to face the privations of the rain forest, either. They were caught, you might say, between the devil and the deep blue sea.

Life at Shawnigan in the 1920s and 1930s was remarkably primitive by our standards. Still, the colonels contrived to maintain among the logged-off stumps and Douglas firs a transplanted British society and a vigorous social calendar. They changed for dinner and talked of *tiffin* and every house on the West Arm Road had its own individual name, usually associated with some family place back home. The Mason Hurleys were no exception. The family seat in Ireland is memorialized in a piece of stationery I still have from those days, printed merely: Glenduffe, Shawnigan Lake, BC. That was quite sufficient address for mail to reach its destination, and

promptly and reliably too.

Although the colonels had their pride and their pretensions, they had very little else. I remember my mother-in-law telling me that when anyone had visitors from home—and in those days, when the journey alone took two weeks, people stayed for several months—other families in the district would rally round and lend silver and anything else necessary to create an impression of affluence.

Leading lights in the social hierarchy were Colonel and Mrs. Eardley-Wilmot. Their huge home, "Knockdrin," named after the family estate in Ireland and surrounded by one hundred acres, towered above the road. "Knockdrin" still stands upon its bluff and has been restored by its present owner. It is now called "Marifield" and the holding is reduced to three-quarters of an acre in the centre of a subdivision. In the Eardley-Wilmots' day the glory of "Knockdrin" was a tea pavilion and two wooden tennis courts, the surface made of two-by-fours. Denis remembered attending their tennis parties when he was a boy. The men wore yellowing white flannels, always held up by an old school tie knotted around the waist. Many wore topees—that tropical pith helmet so reminiscent of the British Raj. In fact, the fashion for topees was sustained by St. George's School in Vancouver, where it was part of the school

Clearing the ground for the grass tennis court.

uniform in 1931 — a grotesque notion on the rain-coast, but the headmaster had taught in Mandalay. The Shawnigan colonels whitened their topees and their tennis shoes, known as "sand shoes," with pipe clay supplied in those days to the army for whitening belts. The women wore white shoes and stockings, bloomers and white skirts and blouses.

History does not relate who made the cucumber sandwiches, but I believe all the ladies helped with the tea, and Mrs. Eardley-Wilmot's ringing English voice could be heard calling to her son, whose name was Vere, "Veah, deah, come heah!" In spite of the acreage, the tennis court and the cucumber sandwiches, my sister-in-law tells me that the Eardley-Wilmots were so poor and had so little fuel that in winter they were obliged to go to bed after supper to keep warm. When they died there was still an enormous mortgage on the property.

Well, of course the Mason Hurleys had to keep up with the Eardley-Wilmots. "Nothing would have it," said Denis, "but we, ourselves, must have a tennis court." Trees were felled, stumps were blasted, a horse and scoop shovel hired, grass seed sown. The result was not exactly a centre-court Wimbledon.

It was said of the colonels that in "Indiah" they had only to drop a pocket handkerchief and a servant would scramble to pick it up. This was certainly not the case at Shawnigan. Each family had only a maid-of-all-work, and dreary was her lot. There was no electricity, oil lamps had to be cleaned and filled daily, water to be pumped by hand, furnace and kitchen stove and boiler all to be stoked with firewood which must be cut down, chopped and stacked.

Denis's father had some ludicrous notion — given his background and total lack of experience — that they could support themselves by farming. They had geese and chickens and pigs. The largest and most stubborn pig was named Mrs. Pankhurst, after the intractable suffragette, and a merry dance she led them. Needless to say, none of this was financially viable or successful.

In the mornings the colonels — some of whose names were Colonel Hall, Colonel De Salis, Colonel Musgrave, Colonel Audain, Colonel Greer, Colonel Prior, Colonel Cheeke, Colonel Kingscote (he was navy), Major McGill and Major Furlonge — forgathered in the village to await the mail on the 10:20 train. The roads in those days were appalling — there was no road completely around the lake — and fleets of small boats used to converge on the government wharf beside the Shawnigan Lake station, which could have been the model for the one in the Provincial Museum, so exactly alike was it.

While the mail was being sorted, the colonels — and their ladies — shopped and gossiped at Kingsley's store. "The Kingsleys," Denis told me, "were real personages in the village. They ran a most excellent old-fashioned, all-purpose general store, down near the railway track, opposite the SLAA Hall. They delivered round the lake by car and by launch, and credit was unlimited. One never paid cash. They were progressive, too. They imported a Delco electrical plant, and were the first people at Shawnigan to have electricity. 'My God, the store's all lit up!'" The Kingsleys had been Koenigs, but changed their name during World War One.

The SLAA (Shawnigan Lake Athletic Association) Hall, which burned down and was rebuilt, was also a social centre. Remittance men (younger, usually unsatisfactory sons of British families, paid by "remittance" to live abroad — who worked on farms in the district joined the colonels at dances held there. Everybody was always properly dressed. Dinner jackets were worn, and on special occasions white ties and medals. In the summer it was white flannels and blazers. The string orchestra played into the small hours when everybody stood rigidly at attention for "God Save the King" before making their weary way home. White flannels and blazers were also *de rigueur* for regatta days. The Shawnigan Regatta was famous in its time, the Esquimalt & Nanaimo Railway adding as many as ten extra cars to the train to bring hundreds of

Boaters in front of the Shawnigan Beach Hotel, ca. 1950.

people up from Victoria to watch the rowing races between the Shawnigan Lake and James Bay Athletic Associations.

Although most houses at Shawnigan did not have electricity, there were telephones—massive instruments on a huge wooden backing with a wooden box containing the mechanism. The wood was the same colour and kind as that used on toilet seats, dark and heavily grained. The mouthpiece on the telephone hung out on a sort of gooseneck, and a hook at the left side held a monstrous heavy receiver. You could easily brain a burglar with it, only there weren't any burglars to brain in those days. Opposite the receiver on the right of the wooden box was a large black metal crank. This you wound round several times to attract the attention of the operator, who sat at a board at Cobble Hill, four miles away. If she did not like you, or did not feel like answering, she ignored your frantic crankings. It was an achievement merely to reach the operator, let alone to complete a phone call. Our number, I remember, was 6Y4, a party line; only businesses were allowed single lines. That meant that when the call was for us, the phone would ring four sharp quick rings in succession. You always

knew, of course, who was receiving or not receiving calls on your line, but honour forbade ever lifting the receiver to listen.

Denis was ten years old in 1920 when his parents arrived from China. He told me that they came to Victoria on the Canadian Pacific liner *Empress of Russia*. Denis remembered as a very small child being on one of those liners when they stopped to coal at some far eastern port and watching a long line of natives carrying baskets of coal on their heads to refuel the ship. After settling in Victoria and making some false starts by buying one or two houses on Beach Drive in Oak Bay, his family purchased Colonel De Salis's house at Shawnigan, promptly changing its name to Glenduffe. The house still stands and has been designated a "heritage home." The present owners have restored the name but, unlike the old days, their address also includes a street number and a postal code.

One of the reasons the Mason Hurleys settled at Shawnigan was that they had two sons to educate and Shawnigan Lake School, founded in 1916, already had something of a reputation. Mr. Lonsdale, however, a great character and an immensely impressive and handsome man, was

The West Arm Road.

enraged and even insulted at the idea that he should be expected to take in anything so plebeian as two *day* boys. Denis said, "When my mother suggested we might board he declared that we could go home only once a term. Since we lived but 300 yards down the road, this my mother would not accept."

She sent the boys to Victoria to board at St. Aiden's School and had them come home to Shawnigan on the train for weekends. Shortly thereafter, the problem was solved by one of Lonsdale's own masters. Mr. Odo Barry defected to set up his own, rival seat of learning. Leinster Preparatory School was established in 1922 in a big rambling house on top of an exceedingly steep hill at the intersection of the Shawnigan and Cobble Hill roads. Denis said: "The school opened with fourteen pupils. We weren't 'students' in those days. I remember Colonel Oldham's children, Stuart and Frankie. There was my brother Pat and myself, and the three Forshaw boys, boarders from Quathiaski Cove on Quadra Island. Our uniforms were sent out from England. Grey flannel—naturally—shorts, shirts and jackets, with a shamrock green, blue and white striped tie, and school caps."

The site of Leinster Preparatory school was not exactly a felicitous choice. Being on so high a hill there was a problem about water. "How well I remember in the dry season we boys in our grey flannel pants and scoop caps carrying heavy pails of water up the steep zigzag track from the lake to the school. We worked in pairs, toting five-gallon coal oil tins slung over a pole, and were expected to make three trips each."

Odo Barry was a remarkable man. He had a wooden leg, a consequence of "the War." Yet with that wooden leg, and supported by a walking stick, he played a better game of soccer than many of his boys. To help him with the school, his mother came out from Ireland. She was a formidable disciplinarian, swathed in voluminous black taffeta. Barry himself was a brilliant teacher, and some of his pupils went on to achieve high academic honours in fields far removed from Shawnigan Lake. Frances Oldham won the Congressional Medal of Honor for stopping the distribution of thalidomide, and Denis's brother Pat became a professor at the Massachusetts Institute of Technology and is cited in *Who's Who in America*.

In fact, Shawnigan became quite an educa-

Glenduffe under construction, ca. 1910.

Mr. and Mrs. F.C. Mason Hurley with Pat (left), Isobel and Denis (right), about 1934.

Glenduffe (in the 1930s) has recently been designated a heritage building.

tion centre. It was 500 feet higher than Victoria, and this was supposed to make the "air" very bracing and healthful. The boys' school, or Lonsdale's as it was always called, continued to flourish in spite of some disastrous fires that from time to time destroyed the buildings. Denis explained: "There was, however, no girls' school, and my mother became concerned about the education of my young sister, Isobel. Then by a stroke of good fortune, she met at a Women's Institute conference at Parksville, Miss Minna Gildea, who was guest speaker. Miss Gildea was an extraordinary woman, passionately devoted to education. My mother pointed out to her that the Canadian Pacific Hotel at Shawnigan was lying empty and for sale (killed by Prohibition) and begged her to start a school, promising her own daughter as the first pupil. Miss Gildea, encouraged in the idea by Mr. Lonsdale, and also by Mrs. Tryon, who had two sons at the school and was president of the Women's Institutes of Vancouver Island, did so." For many years Strathcona Lodge, or "Strath" as it was affectionately known, was one of the most successful (and fashionable) girls' schools in the province. Its proximity to the boys' school, of course, did nothing to detract from its popularity with the young ladies being educated there. New buildings on the site now house the International B'hai school.

There was also a public school in Shawnigan in those days, always known as the "village school" to the colonels who did not consider it suitable for their own refined offspring. It was a one-room affair with an outhouse at the back, situated on the flat ground across the road and at the foot of the hill of the Leinster Preparatory school, and presided over by one teacher. Such are the changes wrought by time that two generations later our own children attended the "village school," by then enlarged, modernized and moved into the village proper. Today a new school is being built in the Shawnigan Lake–Cobble Hill district, the Frances Oldham Kelsey School. It was named in honour of the woman who stopped the sale of thalidomide. The lady herself travelled all the way from Washington DC to the sod-turning ceremonies at age seventy-nine.

There were people at Shawnigan who, unlike the colonels, actually earned their living. On the east side of the lake, where the campground now is located, a sawmill stood for many years. Its shrill whistle blasted forth at 6 a.m. to awaken the employees (as well as those who didn't wish to be woken) and again at seven, the hour at which the workers were supposed to commence work. Its shriek continued at various intervals throughout the day, summoning them to this or that. As a child on vacation at Shawnigan, I remember Sunday as the only peaceful day—the mill employees worked Saturdays too—the only time when one's ears were not assaulted by the scream of the saw and the shriek of the whistle. Such noise pollution would never be tolerated today.

Denis told me that logs for the mill were supplied by a steam tug, *The Lady of the Lake*, a sturdy little vessel whose boiler was fired by slabs of cordwood. It could often be heard throughout the night chuffing across the lake from the log dump on the west side, towing booms for the early shift in the morning. The logs came from the McGee Creek area in the Sooke Hills and were hauled by a logging railway with a Shay sidewinder locomotive. This locomotive is now at the Duncan Forest Museum. In 1944, the mill burned down.

Many a character lived at Shawnigan in those days. Not the least was my father-in-law, F.C. Mason Hurley. After several return trips to Hong Kong, he finally wound up his affairs there, and decided to add on to Glenduffe a room in which to display his large collection of Chinese porcelains. This "museum" was furnished with blue and white T'ien S'ien rugs and ornately carved blackwood Chinese furniture. On the walls hung Chinese plaques and tapestries. There were long narrow windows designed not to let in too much light, a fireplace, a built-in organ and

Regatta Day, outside the railway station, in the 1920s.

glass-fronted cases to show off the magnificent porcelains. Over all presided a Buddha on a stand with a blue crystal light flickering before him. My father-in-law was a great Conan Doylist, a believer in spiritualism, and Denis told me that many a spooky seance was held in this room to the sound of the organ.

Another personage was Judge Hunter, whose magnificent estate on the east side of the lake eventually became Cliffside Preparatory School, now the Easter Seal Camp. Denis remembered Judge Hunter's beautifully polished thirty-five-foot launch, the *Manzanita*, touring the lake with white uniformed and behatted Japanese crew members standing at attention fore and aft while Judge Hunter and his guests disported themselves under an awning at the stern.

Probably the greatest eccentric was old Charlie Armstrong, estranged husband of the Australian diva Nellie Melba, after whom peach

Melba and Melba toast are named. Shawnigan Lake seems a strange destination for such a man, but as a bride in 1940 I remember seeing him often. Denis told me that "Charlie always wore an Australian hat and lived quite alone on a farm, where the west side campground is now. There was no road to his farm, but there he attempted to raise sheep. His house was near the Canadian National railway, a rival track to the CPR on the west side of the lake. The trains were mostly logging and freight trains that ran up to Cowichan Lake, but there was a kind of gas car which could be flagged down for a ride in to Victoria via Sooke and Leechtown. In summer Charlie Armstrong rowed to the village for mail and supplies, but in winter he walked—pack on back—across the ice (the lake nearly always froze then). He carried a twenty-foot pole across his shoulders and when the ice gave way and he fell in—as not infrequently happened—he was able to

Regatta in the village, 1939.

haul himself out again."

About the time the colonels settled at Shawnigan, the summer cottage people began to buy up property also. They were different from the colonels in that they were mostly "Canadian" rather than "British." They were more affluent, too. They bought waterfront and had houses in town as well as cottages at the lake. The wives and children spent July and August at Shawnigan, while the men commuted at weekends up the twisting gravel road over the Malahat. Many of these summer cottages were more like "camps" – without electricity or running water. Indeed, the word "camp" was often used. Others were quite superior, real houses. The names of some of these people were Horton, Grogan, Barclay-Ross, Gregory, Macfarlane, Mayhew, Dorman, Angus. The Anguses even brought a parlourmaid and their Chinese cook up from town with them. In many cases the great grandchildren of the original families still own the properties, still go to Shawnigan in the summers.

In 1927 intimations of financial disaster were looming. One could no longer, it seemed, remain a gentleman of leisure, living off one's capital and hoping to eke out a few more dollars from the likes of Mrs. Pankhurst. Denis said, "My father sold out his CPR shares and bought from Charlie Armstrong a house he owned near Glenduffe. Onto this old house, which had waterfront, he built the Forest Inn." Much of the Chinese blackwood furniture, the blue and white rugs, the Chinese hangings and screens were moved out of Glenduffe to furnish the fifty-foot lounge of the new hotel. Tea was poured from enormous silver pots bought by Denis's father from the P&O steamship line, the initials P&O still engraved upon them. Brasses shone, floors glistened, the waitresses wore black uniforms and white aprons, the guests changed for dinner and the cost of a room, including three meals and afternoon tea, was three dollars a day. The Forest Inn was a very genteel and gentle place: there were no liquor licences in British Columbia in those days. A few years later, during the 1930s, following a motor tour he had taken through the USA, Denis persuaded his parents to change the name – to the everlasting regret of the guests – from Forest Inn to the supposedly more up-market Shawnigan Beach Hotel. As such it remained the family business for thirty-five years, three generations of Hurleys working there. Many of the guest families returned to stay for three generations as well.

The place, which Denis always felt would burn down (the common fate of large wooden buildings in those days), survived through many changes of owner, name and purpose. At one time it was pretentiously designated the Western Canadian College, a boarding school for Chinese students wishing to learn English. Most recently, in the early 1990s, it was called Shawnigan Lake Beach Resort and housed a bar, Spike's Lounge. It was then sold again, and in 1993 it was completely demolished by wreckers. New condominiums will be built on the site.

As for the colonels, what have they left behind? A few family portraits, a little silver, some swords, and fading memories of a way of life long gone.

THE BY-PASS VALVE

Alan Haig-Brown

SHE WAS A GOOD-LOOKING BOAT. Her black hull was just over a hundred feet long, and her white house, big and comfortable, just aft of midships allowed for a large hold forward and a small aft hold. Built in 1943 at San Diego's Terminal Island she was one of many YM something-or-others that had been constructed for wartime use with wartime materials and little concern for their long-term survival. But it seems the materials weren't all that bad and the shipwrights did good joinery in spite of the rush, because in the mid-sixties as she neared the quarter century mark, the *Northern Girl* was showing no signs of age. She now made a 1000-mile weekly round trip carrying general cargo to coastal logging camps from Howe Sound to Seymour Inlet for Logger's Freight Service.

As a young man born in the same decade as

the *Northern Girl*, I was looking for work to fill in time between a winter at university and a summer job on a salmon boat. I had worked as a deckhand a couple of years earlier on another boat for Logger's Freight Service. It was this seniority that determined my position in the five-man crew. One of the other deckhands had just started on the boat so I was given the elevated position of second engineer, which carried no extra pay but put me in limited charge of the engine room on the chief engineer's off-watch. It meant that I would get to start the auxiliary diesel that powered the winch hydraulics when we had to offload freight. I would also charge batteries as required and make periodic checks on the engine's vital signs. "No big deal," thought I, as the Chief explained the big knife switches and showed me how to start the auxiliaries. It was a well-laid-out and brightly lit grey painted space. The two six-cylinder auxiliaries were set forward, one on either side, with a big electrical panel between them. The aft two-thirds of the engine room was dominated by the massive grey twelve-cylinder in-line GM diesel. Putting out a paltry, by modern standards, 500 horsepower, it was the biggest engine I had ever worked around. As we approached it, the Chief pointed to a big tank on the aft bulkhead and yelled over the idling throb of the big diesel, "That's the lube oil tank. This is a dry-base engine and the lube oil is circulated by pump through the engine.

"Now I want to show you the most important part of this job. You see that big brass tachometer on the starboard side? It has marks on it at full, half, and slow RPM. Over here on the port side there is a valve under the deck plate." He bent down and showed me a round hole in the red steel deck plates. Plunging his hand into the opening, he grasped a big valve. "This is the *by-pass valve*. When we are running at full RPM it must be closed so that all the lube oil pumps through the engine. At half speed you have to open it two and a half turns. At slow it has to be open five turns."

Later, over a cup of coffee in the galley, the Chief explained further the crucial importance of the by-pass valve. "I've been on this boat ever

since it's been in Canada. When Logger's Freight bought the boat they got me to come to work for them. These engines were only designed to last 500 hours but I've kept this one going with good maintenance and by paying attention to the by-pass valve. In this dry-base engine it is very easy for the engine to start burning its own lube oil. If the by-pass isn't opened when you slow down and the engine starts to burn its own oil, the revs will just go up and up until the engine blows. When that happens it can blow the whole boat up."

I was impressed and not a little in awe of my enormous responsibility. We left the Arrow Dock in False Creek about 10 p.m. The chief let me watch him setting the by-pass valve as the boat was manoeuvred away from the dock and made her way out through the railway swing-bridge and under the Burrard Bridge. By the time we got up to Long Bay in Howe Sound I was on watch, but the Chief kindly stayed up to give me one more lesson on the crucial setting of the by-pass valve. Open two and a half for half speed and five turns for slow. It wasn't all that scary once you had done it a couple of times.

At Long Bay we picked up a deckload of bundling wires for the booming grounds at Beaver Cove and then pulled out for the run down to the mouth of the inlet and on to our next stop

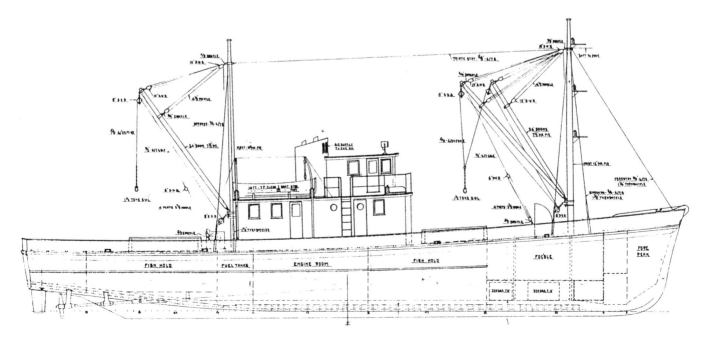

Unloading at Echo Bay.

at the top end of Texada at Vananda. The mate's watch was made up of the mate, the deckhand and me. It was a relaxed wheelhouse regime with us all taking turns holding the wheel and getting coffee for each other. I had just brought up two coffee for the mate and me, the deckhand had gone to check the lashings on the deck cargo as it was blowing a pretty stiff westerly out in the Gulf, and the mate was at the wheel—when we hit the deadhead. There was a bump as it hit the forefoot. The mate grabbed for the throttle and yanked it back to slow. As he did so he turned to me with a look of abject horror and screamed, *"The by-pass valve!"*

"Holy God!" I dove down the ladder from the wheelhouse, leapt two strides down the companionway, grabbed open the engine room door, and slid down the metal rails of the engine room ladder with my feet barely touching the rungs. Clattering to the hole under which the valve lurked I reached in and opened it while counting out the turns, "One, two, three, four, five!"

I looked over at the tachometer. The big needle stayed steady at the lowest mark. The engine was not burning up its lube oil and becoming a wild runaway bent on destroying the whole boat. As the mate kicked the boat back in gear and began to move the throttle forward, I slowly shut the valve back down while I kept a close eye on the tachometer. Real dramatic stuff, but I'd seen lots of World War Two submarine movies with people staring at gauges and turning valves so I knew how to handle it.

By the time I got back up to the wheelhouse the mate had regained his composure. He looked at me and said with a new respect, "Is everything OK in the engine room? Jesus, that valve scares me. I'm glad you know how to work it." I nodded with all the calm self-assurance I could muster. The valve was a damn curse but it imbued the glorified deckhand position of second engineer with more importance than would a sleeve full of gold braid.

Over the next four weeks we made many trips up and down the coast. Each trip comprised sixty-five scheduled stops and a number of unscheduled times when the engine was slowed. I got really good at running up and down ladders and opening the valve. I liked being second engineer.

Things weren't going as well for the Chief. Good crew was hard to get and the Chief got a little rattled the time the new cook pulled a butcher knife on the skipper at the galley table. Maybe he was suffering from home troubles. Working a nonunion job with almost no time at home can be hard on a marriage. Whatever the real cause, he packed his gear off the boat one weekend and said he wouldn't be back.

On loading day I went down to the boat at Granville Island a little early so that I could meet the new Chief. Would he understand all the peculiarities of our unusual engine? When I met him up in the office by the yellow Arrow Freight shed, my heart sank. He wasn't much older than me. How the hell could he know about a World War Two vintage engine?

"Oh hell," he said, "I've worked on every kind of Jimmy diesel there is."

"Would you like me to show you around the engine room?" I offered.

"Sure, I'll be down on the boat a little later."

I went down to the boat and to the now-familiar engine room. I polished the brass rim on the all-important tachometer. Checked the oil level in the big reservoir on the aft bulkhead and waited for my chance to show the new Chief that I knew my stuff. When he eventually came down I showed him the operation of the big knife switches on the electrical control panel. I explained which auxiliary had been rebuilt and so was getting most of the use while the other remained a backup. He gave the main engine a familiar pat and allowed as how he had run one just like it on a stationary generator.

"Well then," said I with a mixture of relief and disappointment, "you know all about the by-pass valve."

"What's that?"

"It's really important," I explained as I thought, "Shit! Where did they find this guy?"

I showed him how to watch the tach and open the valve, then I took him up to the galley and explained how dry-base engines could burn their own lube oil, run away and blow up. It seemed like I didn't explain it right. The new Chief remained unimpressed.

We spent the rest of the day loading the boat. Seymour Inlet freight in first, Drury Inlet, Thompson Sound, Kingcome Inlet, Knight Inlet, Call Inlet, Loughborough and so on. By 10:00 p.m. we were under way. It wasn't my watch, but as the whole crew worked to load the freight, there was always a time as we left port that the watches overlapped. This gave me the excuse to tell the Chief I would go down to the engine room to shut down the auxiliary. It also gave me the chance to do my careful manipulations of the by-pass valve. I got a coffee and went up to the wheelhouse as we came up on Point Atkinson.

"So how's the new Chief?" the skipper asked.

"Says he knows all about this engine," I replied noncommittally.

"I sure hope so. The old Chief had been with this boat an awful long time."

When we neared Long Bay, the skipper's watch went to the galley for a mug-up on their way to their bunks. That first midnight-to-six watch after a weekend in town was always a long one for the mate's watch. We had already put in ten hours sorting and loading freight. I handled the landing at Long Bay and was glad to have breakfast and turn in as we reached the Gulf and set course for Welcome Pass. It seemed like my head had just touched the pillow when I woke to the sound of the slowing engine. I glanced out the porthole and saw that we were coming into Vananda. It was a quick stop and the hydraulics were not needed, so the only reason to go down to the engine room was to open and close the by-pass valve. I listened for the engine room door to open. But there was no sound. I slipped on my pants and crept down the companionway from my cabin to the engine room door. Glancing about, I went below and checked the valve. The big

tachometer indicated minimum revs. I checked the valve. It was still closed! Quickly I thrust my hand into the hole in the deck plate and opened the valve. One, two, three, four, and five. I had saved the boat.

I waited below until the engine speeded up, and reversed the familiar operation. Back to my bunk, and the next stop was at Teakerne Arm. By this time it was noon and the watch was changing. I called to the Chief that I would get the auxiliary and at the same time I turned the by-pass valve. On the mate's afternoon watch we went up Toba Inlet. As I came off watch for my supper I gave the Chief an update on the engine room, carefully mentioning that I had opened and closed the by-pass valve at all the appropriate intervals. "You can do it if you want to," he said, "but it isn't necessary."

The skipper's watch took over as we went through the Yacultas toward Big Bay on Stuart Island. I woke again as the engine slowed for the stop. I began to think how I could get up and turn the valve. But no. Sooner or later I would have to sleep. To hell with it. I'll just see what happens. I listened as the whine of the winches eased into silence and their auxiliary engine was shut down, signalling the end of the offloading. The big diesel revved again as the skipper pushed the boat against the spring line to swing the stern out from the dock. I waited for the big engine to start screaming as its revs cranked the needle off the big tachometer. The revs swung up and down but only in the familiar pattern of manoeuvring a big boat out of a tight dock. Damn that smart-ass new chief was lucky.

Half an hour later the scene was repeated at Shoal Bay, with only a little less violence to my frayed nerves; then at Blind Channel, with the tension easing a little further. I drifted back into a fitful sleep, waking at each stop on the skipper's watch in anticipation of the scream of a runaway engine. I dozed off to images from an old Whalen cartoon I'd seen in a logging magazine that showed pistons coming out through the top of a towboat cabin after an engine had blown up. The more I thought about it, the harder a time I had remembering just what the old Chief had said. He didn't say that it would blow every time the by-pass valve wasn't turned. He didn't even say that he had ever seen one of these engines blow up. I found a little solace in the thought that if the damn thing was going to blow it wouldn't blow when I was in charge.

For the rest of the trip, I continued the ritual of going down to the engine room to open and close the valve on my watch. I sat down beside the big old Jimmy diesel and tried to figure out just what it would look like when it blew, as I still figured it would. At first I woke every time the engine slowed on the skipper's watch. But finally I slept right through. I spent another month on that boat before I left to go salmon fishing. Toward the end there, I was kind of hoping that the damn thing would blow just a little to justify all that running up and down ladders I had done.

I saw the *Northern Girl* several times after that. Once when we were setting our net just below Camp Point, she came booming by just off our stern. The engineer was standing in the cabin door. He gave me a wave and I was sure I could see him laughing. Obviously the engine never did run away on its own lube oil.

I often think of that frantic month I spent flying down companionways and diving down ladders as if my life depended on getting to that by-pass valve. Whenever I get around some old-time engineers I ask about those engines. There were lots of them made with that dry-base lube system, and the old-timers rate them pretty high. Some of them recall the by-pass valve, but I haven't yet met a one of them that recalls having to open and close the damn thing every time they slowed the engine. Maybe this was just one of those old-timey superstitions like not opening a can of milk upside down or not bringing a black suitcase on board the boat. My only comfort is that some men a whole lot older and wiser than I spent a lot more years chasing after that valve than I did.

THE BY-GONE DAYS OF DOLLARTON

Ships loading lumber at the Canadian Robert Dollar Co., 1923.

Sheryl Salloum

THE DISTRICT OF NORTH VAN-
COUVER is an amalgamation of smaller communities, each of which has a particular character and background. The hamlet of Dollarton has disappeared, swallowed up by residential subdivision, but its history is preserved in archival records and the memories of its pioneers.

Development in the area began in the early 1900s as an offshoot of Vancouver's flourishing sawmill industry. One of those mills was the Vancouver Lumber Company. Until 1929 this mill was supplied with rough lumber from its subsidiary on Burrard Inlet, Vancouver Cedar Mills Co., Ltd. (also known as the Cedar Side).

In 1912 an American, Robert Dollar, started the Canadian Robert Dollar Company; in 1916 he built a sawmill and dock in Burrard Inlet next to the Vancouver Cedar mill. According to

Dollar's memoirs, "the Robert Dollar Company moved the terminus of its British Steamship Line from San Francisco to Vancouver, B.C., and in a recent visit I found that we had succeeded beyond our expectations, as our ships were running full of cargo to and from the Orient. . . . We bought 100 acres of land near Roache's [*sic*] Point on Burrard Inlet, six miles from Vancouver and built a modern, up-to-date saw mill. . . . We intended to buy our saw logs, but soon found out that we must buy . . . our own forests and get out our own logs."

The Dollar Mill shipped wood worldwide, and it was common to see large vessels loading lumber at the company's wharf. Charlie Massey worked as an edgerman in the mill and recalls that "most of the logs were twenty to forty feet long, and I put them through a twelve-inch edger. The

68

logs were cut into 12x12 or 12x18 widths; then they were cut into whatever lengths were on the order board. The logs were sent to Japan and were remanufactured in Tokyo." In 1933 Massey was earning a wage of forty cents an hour and notes that the non-Caucasian workers were paid less, fifteen to twenty-five cents an hour.

Commuting to the mills was difficult as there were no bridges linking Vancouver to its north shore. Vehicle traffic from other parts of North Vancouver was made possible in 1918 when the Dollar Road was built to Keith Road (now the Mt. Seymour Parkway). The trip was formidable in terms of time and road conditions, however. The Canadian writer Earle Birney travelled to Deep Cove in the early 1920s and remembers the last few miles of highway as "really a one-way road with passing-places about every half-mile; you had to keep your wheels on mill-planed 'reject' boards, to keep from bogging down in the rain-soaked earth, & be prepared to drive backwards if you met another vehicle." In 1925 the opening of the Second Narrows Bridge increased the highway and rail traffic to North Vancouver, but the route to Dollarton was long and arduous until the opening of the Dollarton Highway in 1930.

Some millworkers rowed across the inlet, some used the service provided by the Harbour Navigation Company, and those living in the nearby village of Deep Cove walked through a trail in the bush. Settlement in the Dollarton area began with mill housing. Robert Dollar found it necessary to "lay out a village, and build houses for our employees; these we consider to be the best working men's houses to be found anywhere. Each house has a garden and the rent of $15.00 a month includes water, electricity and wood. A post office with a daily mail service has been established, which is called Dollarton. Dollarton also has a church, the minister being on our payroll, and a school."

Community old-timers remember that the Dollar Mill houses were designed by Mrs. Dollar. They were much the same, each having five rooms, a shingled exterior, and a big front porch.

Interior of the Canadian Robert Dollar Co., 1923.

Dollar Mill employees' homes, 1939.

Wood-burning stoves were used for heating and cooking. Electricity and wood were originally included with the rent, but were later charged for separately. The prices were reasonable and one former tenant, Charlie Massey, recalls that a truckload of wood cost ninety-five cents in the mid-1930s.

According to early residents, the non-Caucasian workers were not given accommodation on the Dollar Mill site, except in the bunkhouses where only men, not families, could stay. Annie Erichsen worked in the cookhouse. She helped the couple who worked as cooks: "The wife injured her arm and couldn't work, and then the man went out one night and got drunk and didn't make it to work in the mornin'. Someone from the mill came and got me up at half past six, and I had to cook breakfast for fifteen to eighteen men. When the cook came back they fired him and asked me to keep on the job. The men said the meals were more like home-cooked with me doin' it. I worked as cook for a few years.

"I cooked on a big wood stove. I could put six or seven pots on it as well as a big cauldron that I kept for my soup stock. I made meals of roast beef and stuffed roast pork; I made all my own tarts and my own desserts. I had somebody come in and work a couple of hours doin' the dishes. My husband made the beds, and swept the rooms out, in the bunkhouses."

In later years, when the Vancouver Cedar mill closed, the families of the non-Caucasian Dollar millworkers were given accommodation in the Vancouver Cedar mill houses which were smaller and less picturesque, or the men commuted from other areas.

The Roche Point School opened in 1917. The first in the vicinity, the schoolhouse was situated at the southeast corner of Dollar Road and what is now the Dollarton Highway. The one-room structure had two outhouses and was heated by a wood-burning stove. Water was obtained from a nearby spring, and according to Mollie Nye, who attended the school in 1923, "the building had the appearance, with curtains at its five windows, of a house; so much so that a

Chinese vegetable vendor evinced surprise at the answer he got from the teacher that the pupils were not her children!" Besides those from the two mills, several students came from Deep Cove. Rather than walking the trail which linked the two villages, they "would row around to the Dollarton wharf in fine weather."

Amy (Crompton) Bishop taught at the school from 1921 to 1922. She taught "every grade." There were "thirty-nine children . . . as well as two boys who spoke no English—one from India, one from China. Schooling was strictly the 3R's in those days. I remember my Inspector's Report said, 'Miss Crompton is quite properly stressing the essentials.' It was all you could do."

Olive Nye taught at the Roche Point School from 1923 to 1936. Her daughter Mollie recalls that her mother had to instruct "forty children, of many nationalities, in eight grades. Language was a problem with these foreign children because many of them couldn't speak a word of English." As travel to Dollarton was difficult, Olive would "board out in Dollarton until Friday night," spend the weekend at home, and on Sunday evenings return to Dollarton by ferry. "Later on she travelled by bus, morning and evening, and if she missed the bus she had to walk eight and a half miles. In the winter it was very, very trying and cold."

Dollarton teachers also had to deal with health problems. Mollie will "never forget the time that Scarlet Fever broke out in the school. There was also an epidemic of ringworm and many children had their hair shaved right off. . . . . And there were the usual scabies outbreaks and, sometimes, the teachers got it."

The community did what they could to reduce Olive Nye's hardships. According to Mollie, they provided vegetables from their gardens, "sometimes a sack of rice," loads of split wood "piled on her back porch," and "a Japanese lady made her cushions so she could sit down while teaching."

In 1924 a new one-room school was built at the corner of Dollar Road and what is now Fairway Drive. Mollie remembers that "there were no curtains on the windows. There was quite a large playground for the children, and bears often played there as well." By 1926 a second room with a basement had been added. According to Mollie: "It was absolute luxury! It had . . . washrooms and running water! It was a great delight for everybody to go and get drinks out of the tap." In 1963, Sherwood Park School was built above the location of the Roche Point School.

Mollie Nye taught in Dollarton from September 1933 to June 1939. When she started, her salary was $780 a year. "So life was hard, but people were happy. For instance, for a week or two before school quit in June I'd take the children swimming off the dock at the bottom of the Dollar Road. I also remember that the children had school gardens. They raised vegetables and flowers, and they'd reap their harvest in September. It was really a lot of fun for the children. . . . [In 1939] I got the Strathcona prize for the best school in the Inspectorate. It was a small sum of money, and I bought a large picture to put on the wall because we didn't have any nice pictures.

"When I was teaching grades one to four I thought how happy the children would be if they could only have a playhouse. The principal had the [older] boys make a playhouse right in the classroom. It was large enough for the children to walk inside. They had a stove and beds, just like a real little house. It entertained them during recess and noon hours when it was raining. . . . We made a homemade type of store on the counter. Then I thought, 'Now if only I had a phone, they could phone in their orders'; we published a little newspaper to raise the money needed. We ran it off on a jelly pad. That [was like] a small cookie sheet and it had an edge on it about half an inch high. You made a recipe with gelatin and other ingredients—I forget what else went into it. When you finished you had a hard jelly on this cookie sheet. You took your master copy and using a purple pencil, an indelible pencil

Students of the Roche Point school tending their garden, ca. 1934.

Amy (Crompton) Bishop in front of the Dollarton School, ca. 1922.

specially for this, you printed it by hand on a sheet of paper. You then laid it on the jelly pad, rolled each sheet and pulled it off by hand. Then you carefully put on the next sheet. I think our paper usually had four pages. That's about all I had time to do. We sold it for two to four cents, depending on the size. We made enough to buy a toy telephone with batteries. The housewife could then phone in her order to the grocery clerk in the store, and he would make out the bill and deliver the groceries. They learned their arithmetic that way.

"Every year we had Education Week, a time when the mothers and fathers were invited to the school. I would put benches at the back of the room and would go on teaching or, perhaps, put on a little program. Since there were so many little ones, and the mothers didn't always get out for much social life, there was always an undercurrent of parents and toddlers talking while you were trying to teach. But everybody, including the teacher, enjoyed it anyway.

In 1919, Edgar Percy Cummins moved to Dollarton. He developed a deep appreciation for the landscape and stayed until 1966. "I'll tell ya how I happened to go there. When I came back from the war I got a job as a labourer in the Dollar Sawmill. One night my wife and I had a heck of a fight, and I got so damn mad I went out in the middle of the night and went for a walk in the bush. After I'd been out for half a mile or so I saw a light. I figured there was no one surely living out there, Indians [at the Burrard Reserve] were a mile away, and when I got to where the light was, it was the moon, the full moon shining on Burrard Inlet. . . . Oh it was a beautiful sight! I lost all my mad. I went right back and told my wife . . . 'You're not gonna kill me are ya? I haven't got time to do that tonight. We can see about that tomorrow. Come with me.' So she came. . . . Then when I got to the point where I saw the light I stepped to one side. 'Oh, what a wonderful sight,' she said. 'It reminds me of the Mediterranean.' I said, 'That's exactly how it struck me. Listen, you can say yes or no: if I find out who owns all this property and I buy a chunk,

I build a house and build a road to the main road in Dollarton, would you like to live here? Make it a nice big front porch.' And she said yes, so I knew very well that she'd taken to it like I did. Well, in four months the house was up. I bought four acres for the tidy little sum of $400 an acre . . . and we settled down there. We lived in that house for forty-six years."

Some time in the early 1920s Cummins left the mill and undertook the operation of a store on the Dollar mill site. Over the years Cummins also worked as Dollarton's postmaster, justice of the peace, and notary public. Cummins was interested in the development of Dollarton and ran for Council. He remembers that "all the fellas at the mill voted for me and I represented Ward Six . . . for several years. I was Chairman of Finance in the District of North Vancouver for a while." In October 1930, he became part of a special three-person committee appointed by Reeve Fromme to study the high depression-related unemployment in North Vancouver. The committee recommended construction of a highway to Dollarton.

In 1930 Cummins relocated on the new highway, adding a garage and postal service. The "General Store" became a stop for the privately run Deep Cove Stage Lines, and the store became a focal point in the community.

The Dollarton Highway also brought new businesses to the area. In 1930 McKenzie Derrick was founded by J.K. McKenzie, his sons Ralph, Ross and Ken, and his daughter Margaret (Jorgenson). The shipping company, later named McKenzie Barge and Marineways, is still a family endeavour and Ralph's son, Bob, is the president. From 1939 to 1947 McKenzie Barge built warships. After World War Two the company turned to commercial shipbuilding, particularly the construction of tugs and barges. McKenzie Barge was, and still is, a specialist in righting overturned barges.

A small shipyard existed on the property west of McKenzie Barge. In 1949 it was purchased by the Matsumoto family: Philip Ichijuro

Matsumoto and his three sons, Sam (Isamu), Luke, and John. Sam recalls that "the building was old, had mud floors, daylight could be seen through the roofing, and part of the building had caved in from earlier snowfalls. We had to renovate the building before we could get the business started. First we had to get the roofing on and the fastest was to tar paper. It took Dad and I and my two brothers until nine o'clock at night, and all we had was one little lamp to give us light. The next morning there was a foot of snow that lasted to spring! Then we bought the scaffolding and timbers from Burrard Drydock and constructed a building.

"In 1950 we had eight to ten men working for us; some were local, some were from Vancouver, and some were Japanese shipwrights. We started with an order of gillnetters and the orders doubled, tripled, multiplied; we were building thirty-two- and thirty-four-foot gillnetters, and at one point we were building twelve boats every six weeks. We built a ninety-four-foot yacht for John Davis Eaton, fishing boats for New Zealand, a thirty-six-foot vessel for use on Lake Victoria in Uganda, and . . . [a number of] fire-fighting boats for Mexico. In 1960 we pioneered the use of aluminum boat construction. . . . At our peak we had eighty to ninety men employed, . . . [but in 1985 we had only] ten to fifteen due to the bad economy.

In 1988 the company was sold and is now the Pacific Western Shipbuilders Co., Ltd., a subsidiary of Noble Towing.

A second "General Store" opened in Dollarton in 1935. Located on the Dollar mill site, it was operated by Robert Stirrat Junior. In early 1949 Stirrat built a new store on the Dollarton Highway, a few hundred yards northeast of Cummins's store. The new store was operated by Robert Stirrat and his father until it closed in 1968, two years after Cummins's store closed. Mr. Stirrat remembers that there were some extremely cold winters in Dollarton: "In 1948 or 1949 we had a terrible winter that started at the

Matsumoto Shipyards, 1950.

74

Vancouver Cedar Mills Co., Ltd., 1926.

end of September. The temperature went down to ten degrees below zero Fahrenheit and all the trees were frozen at an angle—they were bent over with ice. It stayed cold until March and even the inlet was frozen. A tugboat went down in Burrard Inlet when the ice went through the boat."

Dollarton was a thriving community until 1929 when the Vancouver Cedar Mill and the Dollar Mill shut down due to the onslaught of the Depression. The Vancouver Cedar Mill never reopened and was eventually dismantled. The Dollar Mill reopened in 1932 and operated until 1943 when the mill and its timber rights were sold to the Northwest Bay Logging Company, an H.R. MacMillan (now known as MacMillan Bloedel Ltd.) subsidiary located on Vancouver Island. The new owners closed the mill. In 1944 the property was sold to a local businessman, John R. Sigmore, and his associates. The mill was dismantled and the development of the exclusive Roslyn Park Subdivision was proposed. In the initial phase, the twenty-one homes and fences on the mill site were renovated and painted; two new roads, Roslyn Boulevard and Beach Drive (now Beachview Drive), were constructed. By September 1944, 33 of the 161 lots

had sold: prices ranged from $500 to $1500. Ownership was "restricted to members of the white race," each house had to be "valued" at a minimum of $3000, all houses and vegetation had to "be so placed that they will not interfere with the view of other residents," all purchasers were to receive "a free membership share in the proposed country club," and residents were to have access to the five acres and 1000 feet of waterfront that were to comprise Roslyn Park. The subdivision never reached the stage of development that was advertised. Several lots were sold and a number of new houses built.

In the 1930s, the foreshore between the Dollar Mill and Matsumoto Shipyards became populated with ramshackle cabins built on pilings; these came to be known as "squatters' shacks." The dwellings provided rent-free accommodation for local fishermen, workmen from the mills and McKenzie Barge, and for those in need of shelter due to the Depression. Over the years many shacks came to be used as summer cabins, and by the 1950s approximately ninety lined the beach.

In 1940 the writer, Malcolm Lowry, rented one of the jerry-built cabins for a month's vacation. He and his wife Margerie soon felt that they

Squatters' shacks, Dollarton foreshore.

had found a lifestyle that was "dying out of the world." The Lowrys lived on the Dollarton beach for the better part of the next fourteen years. While there, Lowry completed his masterpiece novel, *Under the Volcano*. A number of Lowry's short stories, particularly "The Forest Path to the Spring," describe Dollarton, as well as life on the beach.

Many of the local people were concerned about what would become of the property in the area of the squatters' shacks. Their view that the shacks were unsightly and the squatters un-desirable was reinforced by newspaper accounts of other Vancouver squatter communities. Van-couver civic officials disapproved of squatters not paying taxes, and an article in the *Vancouver Sun* described the shacks as "unbelievably filthy, disease-breeding, vermin-producing hovels. . . . A nest of perverts."

The local Ratepayers' Association began lobbying to have the area made into a park. In 1949 the Town Planning Commission visited the proposed site and the park was approved. Cates Park, as it is now called, was named after a prominent North Vancouver family which donated property to the site.

The removal of the squatters from the beach became necessary with the proposed construction of the park. The squatters were given eviction notices, and the shacks were bulldozed and burned. The park was not developed until the late 1960s.

Today the mills and the squatters' shacks are gone, but remnants of Dollarton's past remain. The base of the Vancouver Cedar Mill's burner is visible in the southeastern corner of the park. It was long ago dubbed the "Alamo" by the local children who use it as a fort. The area of the old burner is also called "Burner Point" by longtime local residents. The careful observer walking along Beachview Drive and Roslyn Boulevard will be able to spot buildings that were the houses for the Vancouver Cedar and the Dollar mills. Although renovated over the years, a number of the homes look much as they did originally. At the corner of Dollar Road and Beachview Drive stands the Dollar Mill Office. The interior has been remodeled to make it a family home, but the exterior looks much as it did when the building was part of the Dollar Mill.

The landscape has altered dramatically, but in Cates Park one can find aspects of Dollarton that have not changed from bygone days. These are best described in the writings of Malcolm Lowry: the "luminous digladiations" of the Shellburn Refinery, the Roche Point light beacon "standing lonely on its cairn," numerous vessels moving up and down the inlet and "the wash . . . like carved turquoise," "seagulls, returning homeward down the inlet . . . as if shot out of a catapult," "Valkyries of storm-drift" and "the ever reclouding heavens," shadowy paths scented with wild vegetation, "that not merely divide but become the twenty-one paths that lead back to Eden," and "something so still . . . and yet . . .

in constant flow, and in passing on, becomes remote, and having become remote, returns."

Sources and Further Reading

Breit, Harvey and Margerie Lowry, eds. *Selected Letters of Malcolm Lowry*. New York: Lippincott, 1965.

Dollar, Robert. *Memoirs of Robert Dollar*, vol. 2. San Francisco: W.S. Van Cott, 1921.

Lowry, Malcolm. *Hear Us O Lord from Heaven Thy Dwelling Place*. New York: Lippincott, 1961.

——————. *October Ferry to Gabriola*. New York: World, 1970.

Draycott, Walter Mackay. *Early Days in Lynn Valley*. North Vancouver: North Shore Times, 1978.

Interviews with longtime residents of Dollarton, 1985–86.

ONE-ARM WILLY, THE TATTOOED LADY AND THE STRONGMAN

George M. Campbell

SLACK THE HAULBACK AND GO ahead on the mainline, slow. Hoop hoop! B-r-r-r-r-t-t-t! (Pause) Hoop hoop hoop!"

In October 1944 I was high-lead logging at Jeune Landing on the north end of Vancouver Island, working for the Gibson brothers. I was blowing whistles on a slackline yarder. She was a big Vivian diesel running a slack skyline two inches in diameter and fifteen hundred feet long. The line ran to a backspar over a cold deck pile a quarter of a mile away, up a rocky, muddy, miserable, bone-shattering sidehill the like of which can be seen all over this wild, rugged, tree-covered coast. I was fifteen years old. There was nobody in the woods but old men and kids; the rest were away at the war.

That's where I met One-Arm Willy, a wild nineteen-year-old kid with a hook for a hand, punkin' whistles on a sidehill show for the same outfit. William Seminick was his real name. Willy broke me in, that first day in the woods. "Might as well do anything yuh want," he said to me. "The punk always gets blamed fer it anyways." Then he opened up the lunch buckets belonging to the chokermen and rigging slinger that we'd been ordred to gather up and carry on to the hill where the crew would be working that day. He took a piece of pie from one, an apple from another, and replaced these items with a hunk of bark and a rock, respectively. I figured

he was a bit crazy and subsequent events proved me right.

Old Tom Dougherty, the back rigger, used to leave his lunch bucket sitting on a stump halfway down the hill from where he was working. When the donkey puncher blew the noon whistle signalling a half-hour lunch break, Tom would come roaring down the hill, grab his bucket on the fly and skid to a stop beside the punk's fire to eat with the rigging slinger and chokermen. One day Willy took some railway spikes — there were always a few around for spiking guylines — and drove them right through the bottom of old Tom's lunch bucket into the fir stump. Then he carefully replaced the old man's lunch of hardtack and black tea, and waited for the noon whistle.

At twelve noon, Ed Stromberg, the puncher, blew the signal to eat, and right on schedule old Tom came barrelling out of the tree line and down the sidehill, leaping over windfalls and logs as he came. When he got to the stump where his lunch bucket was, he grabbed it as he went by, ripping the top off and spewing hardtack and tea for twenty feet. When he finally got stopped he stood for a moment with the top of his lunch box firmly in his hand, then he looked back to see the bottom still on the stump. And there was One-Arm Willy, standing by the punk's fire, laughing fit to kill.

Willy loved to pull practical jokes, but he hadn't the necessary intelligence to avoid punishment for his pranks. Either that or he just didn't care. Like the time he got into the Aqua Velva late one night and ended up going over to the drying shack and filling up everybody's caulk boots with water. Everybody's but his own. Next morning it was a dead giveaway as to who had done the evil deed, and I reckon the only reason the crew didn't beat him to death is that loggers have a soft spot for the downtrodden, the one-armed and the mentally deficient, and Willy was all three.

Then there was Morris Smart. Morris came into camp as a hooktender. According to him he was the best all-round, long-splice-in-the-main-line, rough, tough, high-balling, snoose-chewing, horny-handed hooktender that ever hit the woods. The only thing he did better and faster than getting the wood to the water was making love to the ladies. There were so many women pining for him in Vancouver that their combined tears would create a high tide clear back to Hope. This was the gospel according to Smart. He stuck around for eight months and I remember when he left, we all went into the drying shack to see him prepare for his trip to town.

He was a big, burly guy, with hair on his chest that ran thick, black and curly from his Adam's apple to his belly button. There he stood in front of a cracked mirror, shaving the hair off his chest into a chipped white enamel basin. Each stroke of the razor revealed another detail of the masterpiece tattooed on his chest. It was a picture of a nude woman, full frontal view, standing with her legs apart and her hands clasped behind her head — a beautiful piece of work, full twelve inches from the top of her curly head to the tips of her pretty toes. Morris shaved off all the hair on his chest except for a bit under each of her arms, and a tiny triangle where her legs met her torso. When he was done he roared, "I'm ready to go to town. Lock up yer daughters and hang onto yer wives!"

And I remember Ed Stromberg too. Ed was the donkey puncher, and he had arms on him like the thighs on an eight-foot Viking warrior. He'd got 'em from pulling the friction levers on that old Vivian diesel. There wasn't a man in camp who could take him wrestling, left or right, though everybody tried. Ed was a quiet man, not much given to playing cards, gambling or talk, but when the saw was pinched he knew what to do.

There were a few of us standing around in the blacksmith-mechanic shop one Sunday, watching Bill Becker, the push, bending tools trying to repair a D8 blade. A husky young second-loader named Buck decided to have Ed on. He picked up an eight-pound sledgehammer that was leaning against the anvil and, grasping it by the end of the handle, he lifted it easily and held it straight out at arm's length.

"Hey Ed," he called to the donkey puncher. "Is Vancouver in that direction?" He remained holding the hammer and pointing with it a good ten seconds before lowering it slowly to the floor.

Ed stepped up beside Buck and gave him a good look over. Then, reaching down and grabbing the anvil by the horn in his right hand, he lifted it up straight-armed, and pointed in the opposite direction. "Nope, Buck," he said quietly, "it's more in that direction."

That's the way it was high-lead logging at Jeune Landing back in 1944. At least, that's the way I remember it.